STOP SQUATTING WITH YOUR SPURS ON

THE POWER TO READ PEOPLE
GET WHAT YOU WANT
AND COMMUNICATE WITHOUT PAIN

Angel Tucker

FIRST EDITION

MORGAN JAMES PUBLISHING • NEW YORK

STOP SQUATTING WITH YOUR SPURS ON

Copyright © 2011 Angel Tucker

ISBN: 978-1-60037-846-1 (Paperback)
Library of Congress Control Number: 2010933818

Published by:
MORGAN JAMES PUBLISHING
1225 Franklin Ave Ste 32
Garden City, NY 11530-1693
Toll Free 800-485-4943
www.MorganJamesPublishing.com

Cover/Interior Design by:
Rachel Lopez
rachel@r2cdesign.com

Contents

Acknowledgements

I thank God for blessing me with a job that I love! I get to change people's lives for the better every day. Who could ask for more than that?

I thank my husband, Dennis, for not only serving our country in the United States Air Force, but for tolerating such a strong **D** personality style and being so supportive of my endeavors.

I thank my children, Danielle, Chase, Hannah, and Elijah, for giving me plenty of material to use as examples in this book.

I thank the team at Bradley Communications. It was through attending your summit in New York that I received the motivation and encouragement I needed to write this book—which I completed in only 30 days! You are doing great things. Keep it up.

I thank Dr. Robert Rohm, of Personality Insights, for granting us permission to print the "Under Control" and "Out of Control" charts in this book.

I thank my editor, Anne Marie Smith, fellow smart-aleck and **D** personality who is just like me and I love her for it! Her husband should be glad that he found such a wonderful woman.

Preface

Personalities. We all have them and we must deal with all types of personalities on a daily basis—unless you are a troll living under a bridge—in every aspect of our lives: parenting, marriage, family, friendships, school, work, and the list goes on.

With some people, you find that you just "click." As soon as you meet them, there is an instant connection. You understand each other and you see eye to eye quickly.

With others though, you may never click at all (at least using your current methods) and you can't explain why. It's not as if the person has done anything to you. For whatever reason, they just rub you the wrong way.

It's my greatest hope that this book becomes an invaluable resource for you. By reading it, you'll learn how to recognize most everyone's personality. "What is the benefit?" you ask. The list is endless. You'll be able to build instant rapport, speak effectively to people, get along with the in-laws, get that job you want, have harmony in the workplace, know a ton about a person before they ever tell you, and anything else that comes from dealing with people.

The bottom line is you'll gain the ability to become bilingual in personalities and create win-win situations. You'll understand how to live proactively instead of reactively.

And the best part? This information is fun, effective, powerful, and easy to use. I hope you come to consider this book your bible for communication. I guarantee it will improve every area of your life.

Enjoy, and welcome to a world of personalities!

Angel Tucker

First Things First

Before you begin to read about the various personality types, I want you to know, first and foremost, that this book is not about putting you or anyone else in a box. And, I am not—and would never—claim that every person of the same personality type is exactly alike. In fact, we are all a combination of four personality types. "Yikes! Does that mean I have multiple personalities?" you may be asking. Sort of. Let me explain...

You are a blend

Eighty percent of the population is dominant in two of the four personality types. What does this mean? Simply put, as you go through this book you'll see much more of yourself in two of the types than you'll see in the other two. Usually one type may describe you a little more than the other, but sometimes they're the same, and that's perfectly okay. This is called your **personality blend**.

You may even see yourself equally in all four types. The point is, there is no right or wrong personality type or blend. Every personality has something to contribute. One is not better than the other—they're simply different. I'll talk more about blends near the end of the book.

Perceptions are well...perceptions

In each chapter that describes a personality type, I've included a section that shows how other personality types may perceive you. Understand that just because someone perceives you to be a certain way, doesn't at all mean that you exhibit any of these traits.

Someone's perception of you is *their* reality, not yours. Often times, we decide whether we like someone before we have ever met them face to face. Maybe we didn't like the way they spoke to us on the phone, or how they walked into the room, or dressed, or sat in a chair. Our perceptions affect the way we interact with people.

About a year ago, I was driving down a street. I glanced in my rear view mirror and saw a woman driving the car behind me. She was quite a distance away, but it appeared that she was smoking a cigarette with her windows rolled up. Now normally, I would think, "Whatever. They're her lungs not mine," but I could tell children were in the car. I became irritated and thought, "Wow! Doesn't she know that she's hurting those kids? If she wants to smoke that's her business, but she has no right endangering children." So, before I even met her, I determined whether I would like her (or not).

I glanced in the mirror a second time and then became unsure if it was a cigarette or something else, such as a pen. "Yes," I thought, "it's a pen. Oh, good." So my perception of her changed instantly to something nicer.

Except…once she was right behind me at a traffic light, I was able to see clearly that it was a cigarette. My perception of her went right back to my initial thoughts.

It's important to understand that if you want to change someone's *reception* of you, you may need to change their *perception* of you. So, in each chapter I will talk about potential misconceptions for your personality type.

> You can't BEWARE of something you are not first AWARE of.

Be careful how you interpret people

Lastly, don't just take a description for a particular personality type and think that you know a person. For example, if you see a man having a great time and laughing, don't automatically assume he is an **I** personality. Maybe he is normally a **C** but is happy because he just got a big fat unexpected paycheck. (You'll understand what I'm talking about later.) The key is to recognize patterns of behavior and not jump to conclusions. You know what they say about assume…

If you get good, though, you can read almost anyone's personality in just 60 seconds. Pretty cool, eh? Imagine the power of influence over relationships and communication you could have. So dive in and have fun learning how different we all are. And when you finish, it's time to let your personality shine!

CHAPTER 2

Understanding the Basics

As I mentioned earlier, there are four basic personality types and that you are a blend of all four. They are:

- **D** (Dominant)
- **I** (Inspiring)
- **S** (Supportive)
- **C** (Cautious)

I've summarized the personalities in the table on the next page.

What's your blend?

Understanding your exact personality blend is very important. To determine your exact blend, I recommend that you take an online personality assessment, which is available on my Web site at **www.personalityprofiles.org**. Click on "Order Materials" and then the "Assessments" button. This assessment will give you a ton of great information about yourself. For now, making an educated guess will be sufficient for determining which two types you are most dominant in.

While you're on the site, check out the great books and other resources that teach more about the different personalities. You'll also find my children's "Four Pals" book series, which teaches kids about our different personalities and helps them accept others for who they are.

Summary of Personality Types

Type	Communication Style	Description	Color	Sign
D	Bottom Line	Outgoing and Task Oriented	Green	!
I	Bottom Line	Outgoing and People Oriented	Red	★
S	A to Z	Reserved and People Oriented	Blue	+/-
C	A to Z	Reserved and Task Oriented	Yellow	?

As in:

Green	=	Money
Red	=	Woo hoo, you get a red star!
Blue	=	Like the morning sky
Yellow	=	Caution
!	=	Action, go!
ê	=	You're the star of the show
+/-	=	Not much bothers them, for the most part
?	=	They question everything

As I mentioned earlier, 80 percent of you will fit comfortably in two of the four groups. The other 20 percent will either be high in just one, high in three of the four, or level. We'll talk more about this later. Again, no type is better than the other; they're simply different. It's important that **all** of them exist. If they didn't, life would be very different.

For example, if we were all **D** types, everyone would want to be the boss, but there would be no one to boss around. If we were all **I** types, the world would be a very fun place, but nothing would ever get done. It's like baseball or football or any other sport; *every* position in the game is important. Everyone has something to contribute. Just think if there were no outfielders in baseball. The game would definitely change.

Do unto others

Learning about your personality type is going to help you understand why certain areas of your life come easy to you, yet other things are more of a struggle or take you outside your comfort zone.

For example, if you are in sales and you are a high **D** or high **I** personality, you prefer to do business differently than if you are a high **S** or a high **C** personality. **D** and **I** personalities prefer to do active marketing. In other words, they're comfortable going after the business. **S** and **C** personalities prefer to do passive marketing. They think to themselves, "I'll just mail them something and if they reject me, I'll never have to know it."

Can you see, already, how our personalities influence our lives? In fact, your personality has everything to do with your income, your future, and your relationships.

And learning about other people's personality types helps you understand the most effective way to communicate with them and how they function the best. Why is this important? Because our natural tendency is to treat everyone the way you would want to be treated if it were you in their situation. You know the saying, "Do unto others as you would have them do unto you?" Many people refer to this as the "golden rule." Well, it's a great rule when it comes to morals and ethics, but not communication. The "golden rule" of communication is this: "Do unto others as they would have you do unto them." Do you see the difference?

Here's an example. Let's say that you are a personality type that likes lots of details and information. You are working with a client that is very bottom line. Your natural tendency is to give the client all the information because that's what you would want if you were the client. In your mind, there is no way to make a good decision without knowing all the information. Unfortunately, your client does not feel the same way. In fact, if you attempt to give them all the information, you'll probably lose them as a client. It's a common occurrence.

You must recognize the personalities you are dealing with so you can provide them with what *they* need in order to create a win-win situation.

Being bilingual gives you the edge

The goal of this book is to give you the tools to become "bilingual" in personalities. Why? People feel a higher trust level with someone they feel understands them and is like them. Understanding the different personalities gives you the ability to adjust your personality "language" and create that trust level. I want you to learn the power of reading people and experience how this can improve every communication endeavor in your life.

To make things happen the way you want them to, you have to understand two things:

1. How and why you do what you do.
2. How and why others do what they do.

This will give you an incredible edge in communication. It can change relationships and even save them. I have helped tens of thousands of people do exactly that. As I travel the country, people constantly share with me how this information changed their lives.

Helping you understand yourself

Another benefit of this book is that it will help you examine your own strengths and challenges. You'll see what you bring to the table and what you may need to avoid. It will help you grow as a person—if you pay attention.

Helping you understand others

This book will also help you understand and, hopefully, have a new appreciation for people that are different from you. Before long, you'll be able to pinpoint the personalities of people in your life. You'll also begin paying attention to their strengths and focusing on what they have to offer instead of what they do that annoys you.

Everyone is wired differently. And if you don't understand this, when someone does something you don't like, you'll believe they're doing it against you or to annoy you. The reality is, they're doing it for themselves.

For example, there is a particular personality that is always late. They have no concept of time. If you don't understand this about them, you'll get upset that they're always late. You would probably think, "If they cared about me at all, they would be on time." The truth is, they probably do care about you; it's just the way they're wired. Understanding this makes it easier to accept those that are different from you.

Improving communication

Another key benefit is that you'll be able to communicate better in both business and personal relationships. This is not just a book for a particular relationship in your life, it's for your whole life. As you read, think about how you can apply this to every relationship you have.

You're both right

Do you think you are always right? If you're a **D**, you do. The reality is, just because you're right doesn't mean someone else is wrong. Take a look at this diagram. What do you see?

Some people see a woman's face; others see Bill Clinton playing the saxophone (okay, it's not really Bill Clinton, but you must admit it looks like him.) Guess what? Neither person is wrong.

The point is, if we would all go through life saying, "I don't see that. Can you show me how you see it?" instead of saying, "I'm right, so you're wrong," just imagine how much we would learn. I believe that everyone is your teacher in some way. Everyone on Earth—even children—knows something you don't. I urge you to be open to learning from whoever can teach you.

Recently, when I shared the woman/saxophone player diagram with a class, one of my students wasn't able to see both images at first. Once I pointed the second one out to him, he exclaimed "Wow!" Isn't that great? If we can just ask others to show us what they see, we could have so many more "wow" moments in our lives. Are you cheating yourself out of "wow" moments by thinking you know everything?

The puzzle of personalities

Personalities are much like puzzle pieces. Each puzzle piece has its own unique shape. So do personalities. No two people are exactly the same. We each consist of our own unique blend.

Think about putting a puzzle together. What is the first thing that you would do after you open the box? Some people may say, "Work on the edges." They're wrong! (Tee-hee, just kidding.) But, there is something that you must do before you do anything. You must first turn the pieces over. You must see the images on every piece before you can begin to know where each fits in.

Likewise, with personalities, you must be able to see each person and their personality before you know where they fit in the big picture. What do they bring to the table? What are their strengths and challenges? How do they need you to communicate with them? All of these questions can be answered just by knowing their dominant personality style.

Different personalities, different reactions

Let's look at how the four personalities would react differently in the same situation…

It's 3 a.m. in a hotel in Louisville, Kentucky and Mr. **D**, Ms. **I**, Miss **S**, and Mr. **C** all jolt awake when they hear people running up and down the halls making loud noises. (It's probably **I**-types doing all the running and noise-making, by the way.)

- Mr. **D** gets up and says something immediately, in a not very nice way.

- Ms. **I** thinks, "There is a party going on somewhere in this hotel and I'm going to find it. Woo hoo!"

- Miss **S** thinks, "Oh my goodness, I'm sure they don't realize how loud they are and how late it is. They must have a good reason. Should I say something? Yes, no, yes, no, yes no."

- Mr. **C** is appalled that they're breaking the rules of the facility.

So, which personality is better? Neither is better or worse than the other, of course. Every one of them has great things to offer. The key is to understand which personality you are dealing with so you can speak their language.

Your house is on fire!

In my workshops, to illustrate how different we are, I ask a volunteer to come to the front of the room. I ask the volunteer (let's call her Susan) to face the wall. I then stand behind Susan, about 50 feet away.

I tell everyone else to look at the projector screen between Susan and me. I tell them to pretend the projector screen is Susan's house and that it's on fire. I need to communicate this to her as quickly as possible, but Susan is deaf.

If I stand there and yell, "Susan, your house is on fire!" will she get the message that I am trying to send? Of course not. It's not that Susan's communication style is any better or worse than mine; it's just different.

My point is that it's *that* different when it comes to how each of the personalities communicate. Each one hears and processes information differently. That's why it's important that you know which personality you are communicating with, so the message you are trying to send is the message received.

So, let's get to it so you can start sending and receiving successfully.

CHAPTER 3

Getting to Know the Dominant D

I absolutely love the **D** personality type—mainly because I'm a **D** myself! This personality type is ambitious, strong-minded, daring, and can be somewhat intimidating. They believe in the motto "Lead, follow, or get the heck out of the way." **D** personalities also:

- Move fast and think fast
- Love to tell people what to do and want things done their way
- Are multitaskers
- Get bored very easily
- Have a strong inner drive to get things done
- Want choices, need a challenge, and want control
- Are very quick to spend money
- Desire large items of quality and power
- Love competition

Sound like any one you know? Maybe it's you—or maybe it's your spouse (or ex-spouse). Unfortunately, many marriages end over misunderstanding various personality types. It's too bad that knowing each other's personality types is not a pre-marital requirement. Many a marriage would be saved!

Let's learn more about the **D** personality.

Blast off

D types tend to have momentary explosions when things don't go their way, leaving everyone else in the room angry or in tears. But once they have their say, they actually feel much better. They're not intentionally hurting others; they're thinking to themselves, "I feel so much better. I'm so glad I did that." The detonation is merely a byproduct of who they are.

D's golden rule

D types, however, are actually very easy to get along with. You just have to live by *their* golden rule: "Do it my way" (thank you, Frank Sinatra).

D is for dreamer

D types are dreamers—and I don't mean day dreamers. I mean make-big-things-happen dreamers. They're always reaching for not just the stars, but for the moon *and* the galaxy. Because of this, they tend to be high achievers and rise to the top quickly. They succeed at almost anything they set their sights on.

That's why it's so important for **D**'s to use their "powers" for good. If you're a **D**, I urge you to "Never cross over to the dark side, Luke." Okay, if you are not a Star Wars fan, you won't get the reference. I'm blaming this one on my husband, the Star Wars geek in the family. (By the way, if you're ever playing a Star Wars trivia game, and you don't know the answer, just guess "Poggle the lesser" and you'll probably get it right. (You can thank me later.)

Don't be late

Are you ever late getting anywhere? Well, **D**'s become extremely annoyed by people who are late. But the funny (and frustrating) thing is, it's okay if *they're* late. That's right, you're not allowed to be late, but they can. What's with that? Well, they say to themselves, "I've got important stuff going on, so *I* can be late, but no one else has a good reason." Crazy, isn't it? You may not agree with it, I know, but it's important that you understand it.

Upfront and open

Another great thing about **D**'s is that you'll never have to wonder what they're thinking. They communicate openly. They're going to tell you how it is. (Okay, I guess there are times when this isn't a great thing.)

However, **D**'s talk more than they listen. They're very blunt and to the point and use a forceful tone. They tend to point their index finger for emphasis and they have a firm handshake. I can't imagine why anyone would be intimidated by a **D**, can you?

It's all about control

The **D** personality type is also very optimistic—as long as they're in control. If they are, then they know everything will turn out fine. And, by the way, you don't have to ask them to take charge. If a **D** shows up at any event, and it appears that no one is in control, they will say to themselves,

"Well, somebody has to be in control here, so it might as well be me." **D**'s feel that they can run anything, whether they know what they're doing or not. They are also quick to take control in times of crisis, so if you're on a plane and it's going down, start praying you have a pilot who's a **D**.

D is also for decision

Have you ever had trouble making a decision? Not if you are a **D**. **D**'s make very quick decisions. In fact, they're irritated by people who don't. They believe that since they can make a quick decision then everyone should be able to do so. This, of course, is a misconception, but it's how they think. They're particularly annoyed if they're waiting on someone else to make a decision before they can continue the project they're working on. So, again, lead, follow, or get out of my way.

Efficient and productive

D's are so good at being efficient that they get more accomplished in the shortest amount of time than any other personality. They know how to get to work right away and gather the things that they need as they go. They don't need everything planned in advance to be productive. Wouldn't it be great if all the personalities were this efficient? (I think so, but maybe that's because I'm a **D**!)

Everything is a task

Another lesson we can learn from the **D**-type is motivation. **D**'s are self-motivated. They don't need others to pick them up off the couch and tell them to get to work. They're already working. In fact, doing tasks is what motivates a **D**. They love getting things done. They live for it. **D**'s often walk around without smiles on their faces, not because they're angry but because they're thinking of everything they need to do. They don't sleep well at night, either, because they're thinking about all the things they need to do as soon as they get up. **D**'s minds are constantly racing with things such as, "I have to pick up the kids, then go work out, then run to the store, then get gas and be at a meeting by noon, then…" You get the idea. Understand that everything to a **D** is a task. **D**'s may not even realize this about themselves (until they read this, of course).

For example, when **D**'s go to a restaurant, they're ready to order as soon as the server steps up to the table. They're hungry and the task is to get full so they can move on to the next task. In fact, they'll usually order the same thing every time they go to a particular restaurant because they know they like it, it accomplishes the task of getting full, then they move on to the next task. (I'll show you how the other personalities approach this same scenario differently in later chapters.)

Being a **D**, sometimes I feel bad that everything in my life is a task and that all I think about is getting stuff done. It can really interfere with relationships. For example, recently, I was in the kitchen when my husband, Dennis, came home from work. He walked into the kitchen and gave me a big hug (he's an **S/I** blend; you'll learn more about him later). While he was hugging me, I was half hugging him back as I looked over his shoulder and thought, "I still need to finish loading the dishwasher. I wish I

> Warning: If you are a **D**, remember, a strength pushed to extremes becomes a weakness.

could reach that plate on the counter and put it away right now. How long is this going to take? I mean it's just a hug and it seems to be lasting forever. I could be getting so much done right now." Yes, really. I was thinking that.

If you are a **D**-type, you can totally identify with me. If you are not, you are probably shaking your head and thinking, "That's so sad." I agree, it's sad not being able to enjoy the moment, but that's a **D** for you. It's all about the tasks.

Results, results, results

D's also are results-oriented. They want results and focus on overcoming all opposition to get them. **D** also could stand for "dogmatic" because they let nothing get in their way when they set their sights on something. Their mantra? "Never say die!"

They want to see the fruits of their labor constantly, because they measure success by what they can see. This motivates them to produce more results. More results equal more tasks, and more tasks equal more results…the cycle is endless.

New and improved

One of the things they love to do is look for new and better ways to do things. I guarantee the person that thought of putting wheels on luggage was a **D**. For years we dragged heavy suitcases around until a **D** finally exclaimed, "Duh, roll it!" Most of us then threw out our old luggage and got new rolling luggage. Other personality types, however, handled this a little differently; I'll talk about this in a later chapter.

"No" means "ask again later"

If you haven't figured it out yet, **D**-types are very persistent. They don't accept rejection. In fact, the word "no" simply means "ask again later."

Boredom is excruciating

D's bore easily. They can't stand to sit around and do nothing. They need constant stimulation and activity. They love to stay busy and, if they aren't, they will create something to do. As a **D** myself, sometimes I think, "I can't wait until I can just do nothing. I want to sit down and relax for hours." The reality is, that would bore me to tears. I have tried it for about five minutes at a time and it's painful. Boredom and sitting still actually causes me (and most other **D**'s) stress thinking about all the tasks I could get done if I weren't just sitting there.

Jugglers

D's are also good at juggling priorities. Because they need so much going on at a time to keep from getting bored, they tend to have a lot of balls in the air at one time, and are able to juggle them like a pro. They also keep track of all of them and know which ones are the most important.

Just let *me* do it

Although **D**'s like to get a lot of stuff done, they prefer to work alone. To them, working with someone else slows them down. They think, "By the time I show you how to do it, I could have just done it myself." And they also believe that if they do it all by themselves, it will get done the way they want it done.

Heroes that save the day

D-types are very good at coming to the rescue when they think some sort of injustice has occurred. They love political issues and "save the whales" agendas. They love to be the hero that sweeps in and uses their strategies and expertise to save everyone. Ta da, **D** to the rescue once again (at least in their own minds anyway).

By the way **D**'s, this is an appropriate time to point out to you that there are two things I know for sure:

1. There is a God.

2. It isn't you!

Ha! I couldn't resist. I would say I'm sorry, but I wouldn't mean it since I'm a **D**.

Know it alls

"I know it all," says the **D** to him or herself frequently. Yes, they actually do think they know everything, whether they do or not. And if they're wrong, they have to be proven wrong—in writing. It's very difficult to convince a **D**-type that they're incorrect. Don't give up on them though, just use logic and they will come around eventually…maybe.

Quick witted

D's are very quick witted. I have a friend whose last name is Crook. She and her husband were visiting me when I lived in Washington, D.C. They went to church with me, and I introduced them to the pastor as Dale and Susan Crook. As the pastor politely shook Dale's hand, Susan asked, "Do you have a prison ministry?" How hilarious is that? The only thing I was upset about was that I didn't think of it first.

Logical not emotional

D's are not very emotional beings. They make decisions based on logic, not emotion. Because of this, they may appear very unemotional or unfeeling to other personality types (more about that later).

D's love a challenge

Want a **D** to do something that is on *your* agenda? Here's a tip that may be worth what you paid for this book. The way to get a **D** to do something every time is to simply challenge them. If you tell a **D** they can't do something, they immediately think, "Don't tell me I can't do that." Even if they didn't want to do it before, they'll do it now.

Here's how to use this to your benefit. Let's say that you need your house painted. Here's what you say to a **D**: "There is no way you can paint this entire house in two days. I'll do it myself so it gets done." Then you start painting the house—differently than you know they would. They'll respond with something like, "Don't tell me I can't paint a house in two days. I'll paint both our house and the neighbors in a day and a half. I don't even need *your* stinking two days."

Isn't that great? Trust me, this works wonders, especially with **D**-type kids.

Time is money

Because time is money to a **D**, they move quickly. They walk fast and with heavy feet. You can easily pick out **D**'s on the corner of a busy street. They're the ones tapping their foot, acting impatient, and stepping into the cross walk before the light changes. Because, of course, that extra .2 seconds is going to get them there faster, right? You also know when a **D**-type comes into your office. A **D** is like a tornado that sweeps through leaving wreckage in its path.

Quantity not quality

D's are not worried about perfection, however. To them it's all about quantity, not quality. Unlike some of the other personalities, for a **D** "good enough" is good enough. They do not waste time trying to get it just right.

What's in their closet?

If you get really good, you can often tell someone's personality just by the way they dress. **D**'s tend to dress in no-nonsense name brand clothes. They often wear a lot of black. They do *not* like clothes with ruffles, lace, or bows (it makes *me* physically nauseous to even think about wearing something so foo-foo).

D's keep jewelry to a minimum. The jewelry they do wear is usually the jewelry they have on all the time (unless you also have a high **I** trait, which we'll talk about later in the book).

D's almost always wear comfortable shoes. They're typically on their feet a lot and know that if they aren't comfy, they won't be able to accomplish as many tasks.

Quick thinkers

D's are good at spotting the practical answers to life's challenges. They find it hard to understand why everyone else doesn't see the same answer they do. Years ago, when I worked for a retail chain, I received an evaluation that said, "Has no patience for stupid people." That's actually what it said!

Of course, other personalities aren't stupid, but a **D** may assume they are if they don't think as quickly as them. It's essential for **D**'s to remember and understand that *everyone* is important.

Organized chaos

D's are organized in a way that doesn't appear organized to some of the other personalities. Their desk is an absolute mess, but they know where everything is. They can call someone on the phone and say something like, "Can you go into my office and get a phone number for me? It's on a blue piece of paper in the big stack on the right, about four pieces from the bottom."

I's, who we'll discuss next, have the same trait. They both are "out of sight, out of mind" processors. Whatever it is must be in sight or it will never get done. They are "pilers," both at home and at work, so they can physically see and not forget things. For example, whenever I'm traveling you'll know it, because my kitchen counter is covered with items that I need to pack. I usually start the day before and, as I remember things I want to take with me, I add them to the pile. **D**'s and **I**'s will put things with their car keys, their wallet or purse, or in front of the door so they don't forget them.

Post-it notes are also something **D**'s and **I**'s have in common. They both love to use them and have them everywhere. If you see someone's office scattered with post-it notes, rest assured, they're either a **D** or an **I**.

Likewise, **D**'s and **I**'s both clean house as though they have ADD (Attention Deficit Disorder). They don't clean one entire room and then move to the next room. They're all over the place: make the kids bed, put the clothes in the wash, take out the garbage, clean out the car, put the clothes in the dryer, clean the counters in the bathroom…you get the idea.

During one of my seminars, an attendee actually ran from the room to call his wife after I explained this. He said, "I finally know why I clean the house the way I do—and it doesn't mean anything is wrong with me." I love when people have revelations like this!

You must need something to do…

Remember how I said earlier that **D**'s like to accomplish tasks? Well, they assume that *everyone* is wired this way. In fact, if they're working and someone else is not working, they feel like that person needs something to do. They think, "They must be bored doing nothing. I'll help them out and give them something to do."

The challenge, however, is that they have trouble letting go of control and will usually assign only menial tasks such as arranging chairs, making phone calls, or greeting people at the door. They must keep the important things for themselves.

Clear and concise

The **D**'s "time is money" attitude is reflected in their writing style, whether in an e-mail, a text message, or on paper. **D**'s will use as few words as possible. Their goal is to get their message across quickly and move on to the next task.

The following is a great example of a **D** note:

> Amy,
>
> DO NOT touch the walls!
>
> There is <u>wet paint</u>!!!!!
>
> Angel

Here's how you can tell:

- They did not write "Dear" before "Amy." That would be the waste of a word.
- They used CAPITAL LETTERS for emphasis.
- They <u>underline</u> words for <u>power</u> and <u>emphasis</u>. By the way, if you see someone's signature and it's underlined, They're most likely a **D**.
- They love to use exclamation points! This is to let you know that they're serious about whatever they're saying!!!!
- They did not write "Sincerely, "Love," or "Regards" before their name. Again, why waste a word?

If someone sends you an e-mail and they don't begin the message with your name, he or she is probably a **D**. They think, "Well, they should already know who I'm writing to since I sent it to them."

By the way, it's very important that you understand the other person's personality you are writing to. If you don't, you'll communicate with them in your personality style and may not get your message across.

For example, if you are very detail oriented and send a **D** a long e-mail with four pages of text, you may lose them after the first paragraph. I'll talk about how to communicate with a **D** in a later chapter.

Don't take it personally

D's are more interested in achieving goals than in pleasing people.

> You need to have thick skin to hang around a **D** or you may get nicked!

It's important to understand that **D**'s do not stand around wasting time chatting about their weekend in the break room on Monday mornings. They're not interested in socializing when tasks are out there waiting to be performed. So, anything you want to tell them that's not helping them complete a task is, unfortunately, something they're usually not interested in hearing. They really don't want to hear about your granny, or your dog, or about what you did last Friday night, because none of that information makes them money or helps to accomplish their goals.

This may seem mean to anyone who is not a high **D**-type, but it's just the way they are—so don't take it personally. Again, to **D**'s time is money and, at the end of the day, they know they cannot get their time back.

And by the way, if a **D** is giving you their time, appreciate it because it's the most valuable thing they have.

Beware of the lion

D's also don't tolerate weakness in others. They can sense weakness from a mile away and will devour anyone they perceive as weak. So be careful around a **D**—you don't want to get too close to their cage if you don't know how to handle lions. They *will* bite!

Crooked pictures

The great thing about knowing all this wonderful information is that you can learn how to mess with people. (I'm sick, I know, because I find this quite entertaining sometimes when I'm bored or feeling kind of **I**).

For example, **D**-types usually cannot stand to see a picture on a wall crooked. When they do, they'll drop everything and straighten it. It's an obsession. So if you have a **D** coming to your house and want to amuse yourself, adjust all of your pictures so they're slightly crooked, and then sit back and watch. It's hysterical.

There is, however, one personality type I avoid messing with, and that is the **S**. Why? When I talk about the **S**-type in a later chapter you'll see but, in a nutshell, they're just so darn sweet. And I'm pretty sure that you go straight to H-E-double hockey sticks for messing with an **S**. (If you don't understand what that says, read it again. You'll get it sooner or later.)

Clues to recognize D's

To sum it up, here are some clues that will help you recognize a **D**. They:

- Find it hard to relax

- Often talk with their hands

- Sit on the edge of the chair waiting for action, usually leaning forward

- Want conversation to be on business or on solving a problem

- Reach for something they want without asking permission to use it

- Know everything about every subject

- Talk down to others

This personality type can be difficult, but they are the movers and shakers of the world with things to do, places to go, and people to see.

Do you know a **D**? Maybe it's you. If so, pay attention to the next chapter, which describes the potential pitfalls of being a **D**.

CHAPTER 4

The Challenging Side of the D

A re you starting to recall a few **D**'s you know? I bet there are at least a few of them in your life. As you read, you'll see that there are many great things about being a **D**. I, personally, quite enjoy it! Unfortunately, there are some people that are annoyed by our **D**-ness. They think **D**'s are bossy, abrasive, cocky, egotistical, uncaring, loud, obnoxious, stand-offish know-it-alls. Bummer.

But, again, just because some people think you are these things doesn't necessarily mean you are. But the truth is, if you are a high **D**, at least one or two of those words probably apply to you (hey, don't kill the messenger).

Another important thing to understand about personalities, is that they can be very different depending on whether they're under control or out of control. As I said before, a strength pushed to extremes can become a weakness.

Let's do a quick self assessment. Which of the two words in each column in the following table do you think apply to you the most?

Under Control	Out of Control
Courageous	Reckless
Quick to respond	Rude
Goal-oriented	Impatient
Deliberate	Dictatorial
Self-confident	Conceited
Direct	Offensive
Self-reliant	Arrogant
Straightforward	Abrasive
Competitive	Ruthless

Did you choose some of the "Out of Control" words? The biggest challenge for **D**'s is that they refuse to believe that they have any challenges. They don't know how anything about them could be the least bit offensive. The reality is that we *all* have pitfalls that we should be aware of.

All work and no play...

Remember, no one lays on their deathbed thinking, "I wish I could have worked more."

D's are compulsive workers. When they're at work, they feel bad that they're not at home. When they're home, they feel bad they're not at work.

D's, take some advice and take the pressure off of yourself and the other 90 percent of the population that doesn't function like you. Relax...without feeling guilty. Plan leisure activities. Take time to smell the roses (or at least notice them).

This doesn't involve, by the way, taking your crackberry, your laptop, your cell phone, and every other technology item with you. That is simply working in a different location.

Don't bother, I already tried that

As I said in the previous chapter, **D**'s believe that since they're right (or believe they are), then the other person must be wrong. And that is…wrong.

I heard a story about a doctor who was traveling on a country road in Texas. His car slid off the road and became stuck in the mud. He tried for a very long time to get it out with no luck. Eventually a 19-year-old boy came along in a pick-up truck. He asked, "Do you want me to get your car out of the mud?" The man replied, "Don't bother. I've been trying for a while. It's good and stuck and is not going to budge." The young man hopped in the car, rocked it back and forth a few times and, in a few seconds the doctor's car was out of the mud.

The point is, if we would all go through life saying, "I don't see that. Can you show me how you see it?" instead of saying, "I'm right, so you're wrong," just imagine how much we would learn. Let someone else be right once or twice. Learn to apologize. Admit that you have a few faults. Everyone knows at least one thing that you don't, so always be open to learning.

Tone it down

D's are too blunt for many people. They need to tone down their approach and not come on so strong and overbearing. Remember, the perception that other people have of you is their reality.

Listening but not hearing

D's are not good at "being present," particularly in personal relationships. Many times, if someone asks, "Can I talk to you?" they say, "Sure, go ahead. I'm listening," as they check their e-mail, text messages, and voicemail. They must learn to pay attention to just one thing or one person at a time.

Lopsided wheels

Balance is key for a **D**. They must work to establish balance in every dimension of their lives: physical, spiritual, family, work, and so on.

Picture each of these dimensions as separate sections of a wagon wheel. **D**'s tend to have lopsided wheels because they focus on only one or two areas to an extreme instead of staying in balance. This, of course, uses more energy—just as it would if you were driving a stage coach with lopsided wheels. Eventually, something has to give.

Control freaks

"Do what you do best and delegate the rest!" is the motto of the founder and CEO of a major real estate franchise. He's right. And this is a lesson that **D** types need to learn.

D's have trouble letting go of control. They feel they must do everything themselves. But ask yourself:

- What do you really enjoy doing?
- What are you best at doing?

Focus on these things and delegate the rest. This will also help you get that wagon wheel in balance.

Planning versus enjoying

When **D**'s are at Point A, the only thing they can focus on is Point B. And then, when they get to Point B, they still aren't happy because now they're focusing on Point C.

> **D**'s must learn how to enjoy the journey along the way or they'll miss out on so much in life.

D's, have you ever noticed that you get more enjoyment out of planning your vacation than you do being *on* your vacation? You have already envisioned and enjoyed the entire trip in your mind, so when you actually get there it's as though you've already done it all.

Fast talkers

Another challenge for both **D** and **I** personalities is that they tend to talk very quickly so that sometimes **S** and **C** personalities can't keep up.

Recently, I was speaking at an engagement in Atlanta. A gentleman, who was receiving an award, was good-naturedly asked by a **D** in the audience, "Where's your tie you were gonna wear?" Unfortunately, the person spoke so quickly, everyone else in the audience heard, "Where's your tiger underwear?"

Do you see how this might cause problems for **D**'s?

Definitely not a softie

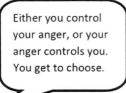

Either you control your anger, or your anger controls you. You get to choose.

D's also have trouble being sensitive to the needs of others. They are not compassionate in nature. They figure, "You got yourself into that mess, you can get yourself out."

As a **D** myself, I can show compassion when I feel that someone is in a position that is out of their control, particularly children. But if I know that it's your own fault, it's very difficult for me to empathize. Brutal, huh?

Quick to anger

If you are a **D**—and you are being honest—you'll admit that you tend to anger easily. Please understand this about anger: it destroys the vessel that contains it. That vessel is you. I challenge you to evaluate the result of your anger. Does it make your life better or worse? The answer is obvious, right? But if it's so obvious, why do **D**-types anger so quickly?

The great news is that anger is a choice. Here's is an illustration. Let's say that you are in a heated argument with your spouse. You may be calling them names and making sure they know exactly what you think of them. During the argument, your phone rings. You answer the phone with a joyful, "Hello!"

Guess what? You made a conscious decision to be angry with your spouse, but not the person on the phone. Isn't it wonderful that you can control your anger if you choose to?

Hard to please

The **D** personality type is also very demanding and hard to please. There is nothing wrong with asking others to do things, but be careful how you ask. Are you rubbing people the wrong way? Do they view you as a tyrant?

Remember, there is often more than one correct way to do something. Don't be so hard to please. Just because someone isn't doing it *your* way, ask yourself if the end result will still be the same if they do it their way. If it will, then let it be.

More challenges for D's

D-types have a difficult role in life. They have the answers, they know what to do, they make quick decisions, and they can bail others out, but they're rarely popular because their assurance and assertiveness make other personality types feel insecure.

D's carry themselves with such assurance that other personalities think that they look down on them. That's why **D**'s must be careful about coming on too strong when dealing with other personalities. **D**'s also:

- Are not good at detail work unless they have a high **C** trait (we'll talk about **C**'s in a later chapter)
- Tend to be "situational listeners." If it benefits them, they're all ears. Otherwise, they didn't even hear what the person said. All they hear is, "Blah, blah, blah, blah."
- Have pre-determined solutions for problems. If someone is explaining a problem they're probably thinking, "Would you shut up already? I already know how I'm going to fix it."

- Tend to be bad on follow up
- Make snap decisions
- Don't like teamwork—unless they're in charge of the team
- Break policy and procedure (to a **D**, the speed limits are merely a suggestion and it's only illegal if they get caught)
- Must be in control (to a fault)
- Don't know how to handle people well
- Interrupt frequently
- Are defiant
- Must win every situation
- Are argumentative and impatient
- Try to intimidate others to get their way
- Hear, "Do you want to fight?" when you tell them to do something
- Tend to have a short fuse and a hot temper
- Feel comfortable with conflict or war

Be constructive, not critical

D's have the mindset that if they tell people they're doing a great job, they're going to slack off. "Great job!" is something **D**'s need to learn to say to others—often. They must be careful about treating everyone in their life as if they're running a boot camp.

Also, be sure to praise in public, but criticize in private. Few things are more damaging to a relationship than public humiliation. If what you have to say is constructive or critical, say it behind a closed door.

Chill out

D's have more self-imposed stress than any other personality type. They have already decided the way things should go and, if they don't go that way, they get upset. The funny thing is that they get upset even if it doesn't matter whether it goes that way or not. For example, **D**'s become angry if they decide that they want to leave the house at 5 p.m. to go to dinner, and its 5:02 p.m. and the kids are still getting into the car.

As a **D**, I try to live my life using two pragmatic thoughts:

- It is what it is.
- Will it matter in ten years?

I cannot tell you how many times I have shown up at a car rental counter to pick up the car I reserved and there are no cars left. Or, how many times a hotel where I reserved a room doesn't have any rooms left when I arrive at midnight after flying all day. Or, how many hours I waited for a flight, only for it to be cancelled.

It is what it is. What can I do about it? Is standing there pitching a fit or cursing someone else out going to change anything? No. What it *will* do is make me more upset and the other person miserable, so what's the point?

Will it matter in ten years? The truth is, most things won't matter in ten days much less ten years. **D**-types tend to make a big deal over everything. We must learn to choose our battles. We cannot control everything. We need to chill out.

Smile

Smile. It works wonders.

- When someone has upset you, or you feel like you want to tell someone off, smile.
- Before you even start talking to someone, smile.
- When someone approaches you to ask a question or make a comment, smile.

Grins win. It's hard for someone to be mad at you if you have a genuine smile on your face. Think of all the time you'll save by eliminating fights. Remember, time is money…

Improve your life and the lives of others

If you see yourself in many of the characteristics I described in both this and the last chapter, then you are probably a high **D**. And, if you are, hopefully you noticed a few things that you could improve on.

You have so many positive things to offer, so don't become consumed with the negatives. You cannot operate under both a positive and a negative at the same time. You'll improve both your life and the lives of those you touch every day by:

- Learning to respond to the leadership of others
- Looking up to and not down upon others
- Not manipulating people when you are not getting your way
- Working on finding more patience
- Not giving advice unless you are asked for it (ouch)

- Waiting for the other person to stop talking before you speak (quit interrupting)

D affirmations

I love affirmations. In fact, I say them with my son every night before he goes to bed because it gives him positive things to think about. Here are some great affirmations for you **D**-types:

- I am caring and compassionate.
- I consider the feelings of others in everything I do.
- I look at both sides of every situation before making a decision.
- I value the input of others.
- Everyone is my teacher that I can learn valuable lessons from.
- I enjoy spending time with others.
- I love to relax.

I recommend writing them down three times at the start of each day. Feel free to come up with your own and add to this list.

Remember **D**'s, stay within your strengths and, by default, your challenges will be minimized. Focus on being the words in the "Under Control" column listed at the beginning of this chapter. If you do, then everyone around you will see what great attributes you bring to the table, and you'll have an unbelievable following.

CHAPTER 5

Getting to Know the Inspiring I

O h, how I love the **I**-type! This world would be such a boring place without them. **I** is my second highest personality trait, so I can certainly identify with **I**-types. Here are some things you should know about them:

- Life is a series of quick ups and downs. They may be happy one minute and in tears the next.

- Things are either really good or really bad—there is nothing in between.

- They're great at persuading and motivating others.

- They move very quickly.

- They're the funniest people they know; they can laugh at themselves for hours.

> Don't you just love them already? If you are an **I**, you are thinking, "Actually, yes, I *do* love me."

See the shiny object?

Recently, a friend of mine said something to me that demonstrates an **I** perfectly. She said, "I intended to conquer the world until I saw

43

something shiny." This personality type is easily distracted and will jump from thing to thing depending on what they're most interested in at the time and what seems the most exciting.

I's are enthusiastic over just about anything. All they have to hear someone say is, "Do you want to go…?" and they will immediately exclaim, "Yes!" before you have said where you're going. They want to go and do and be a part of as many things as possible.

They want to be involved in every conversation around them. They have a unique talent because they can actually hear every conversation in a room and will instantly join the conversation that they find the most interesting. What does this mean? Well, you may be talking to an **I** and, when you turn around, they may have moved on to a conversation they found more interesting than yours. Don't take it personally, they just saw something shiny.

Let go of my arm!

Have you ever had someone physically hold on to you while they talk to you? If so, it's an **I**. They do this because they don't want you to get away before they finish their story. It's amusing to watch a conversation between a **D** and an **I**. The **D**-type actually tries to get away. They slowly start walking out of the room or to a different area. The funny thing is, an **I** has no idea the **D** is trying to get away. The **I** just assumes the **D** wants to talk somewhere else, so they follow them.

I have an **I**-type in my family who thinks nothing of following someone to the bathroom and standing there until the person comes out so they can pick up the conversation right where they left off. (or just keep talking to you through the door) They honestly have no idea that the other person is done talking.

I'm here! Let the fun begin

For I's, life's a good time. They believe that if you can't be with the one you love, just love the one you're with. This personality loves to be the life of the party. In fact, they

> I's like for people to talk about them— whether it's good or bad. They're just thrilled that the person knows who they are!

take the party with them everywhere they go. They never want to enter a room unnoticed. They enter as if to say, "I'm here, let the fun begin." And I's never worry about going to a party, like some other personality types, because they can blend, like chameleons, into any environment in order to have a great time.

I's are the easiest to spot in a crowd. They tend to have naturally loud voices. You usually hear them before you see them. They often enter a room with hugs, kisses, shrieks, and laughter. They enjoy being the center of attention.

I's seeks interaction and recognition. They want you to get excited over their clothes, hair, make-up, jewelry, car, and everything else. They love to banter back and forth with others, and they crave public "Atta boys!"

I'm bored

I's never sit still. Remember how I said that D's get bored easily? So do I's. In fact, just watch them. They move, jump, wave, and wiggle. If they get bored, they will start doodling or coloring in the "o" letters on their paper when they're in a seminar or class setting.

Hugs and kisses

If you've ever seen someone that hugs and kisses every person around them, you've seen an **I**. You can usually spot them coming from a mile away, hugging and kissing as they go. I'm pretty sure every church automatically comes with an **I**. They also love for others to hug and kiss them, so don't be shy, smooch away!

Smiley and bubbly

This personality is also fast-paced and moves very quickly. They're outgoing, animated, and smiley. If you notice someone who walks around with a big smile, and he or she is also bubbly, that person is most likely an **I**.

> **D**'s and **C**'s often think this behavior is obnoxious. Maybe they could use a little more smiley and bubbly in their lives!

Other people usually have one of two reactions to a smiley and bubbly **I**: they become upbeat themselves or they become really annoyed.

People motivated

I personalities could care less about accomplishing tasks. They're motivated by and love being around people. In a previous chapter, I talked about the **D** being ready to order as soon as the waitress comes over in a restaurant. Well, an **I** doesn't even *look* at the menu until the waitress walks up. Why? To an **I**, it's not about the eating, it's about having fun and being with friends. Eating is just something to do while socializing.

Flashy dressers

Have you ever seen someone decorate his or her car for Christmas? Maybe they had a wreath hanging on the front, or reindeer ears extending from each window. Guess what personality they are? See, you are getting good at this already!

I's love to dress for the occasion; flashing light bulb earrings at Christmas time, vests with pumpkins at Halloween. They jump into whatever season it may be—wardrobe first.

They also have a different mindset when it comes to shoes. D's, as I mentioned, buy shoes for comfort. I-types just want them to look good. It doesn't matter how uncomfortable the shoes are, as long as they look stylish. Looking good is worth the pain and future bunions.

They also make purchases based on colors, trends, and uniqueness. They get excited when their purse matches their shoes, their earrings, and their dress. If they're shopping for a home, they might buy a house because they like the flower bed by the front porch, or because they love the current owner's furniture—even if it isn't staying with the house.

I women carry two types of purses:

- A mother purse
- Baby purses

The I uses her mother purse to hold her baby purses. If you look inside a mother purse, you'll see what I mean. The mother purse is usually very colorful with large leather circles, sequins, animal prints, or even their initials (so they don't forget whose purse it is). Baby purses are used for quick trips into the store.

On one of my many travels, I saw a young woman, about 19-years-old, in the Atlanta airport carrying a purse that would normally have been an **S** purse—the kind that has about nine see-through slots on each side. Normally, an **S** would get a purse like this and put pictures of their kids, grand kids, or pets in the slots so everyone could see them. I knew the young woman, in this case, was an **I** though because every single picture was of her. That's right, eighteen pictures of she, herself, and her—at the prom, with friends, at gymnastics. That's an **I** for you.

I still remember going to Sea World with my family several years ago. My oldest child, who is a high **I**, saw a man drawing caricatures. She asked if she could use her money to have a picture drawn. My husband and I said, "Sure," assuming that she wanted one of the entire family. I guess we shouldn't have been so surprised when she wanted one of just her. Yep, that's our sweet **I**.

Pssst! Want to know a secret?

As I mentioned previously, one of the great things about understanding different personality types is knowing how to mess with them. Here is how you mess with an **I**: pretend that you have a secret. Secrets drive them absolutely crazy. They will take you to lunch, buy you gifts, and do whatever else it takes to find out your secret. Fun, huh?

Talk, talk, talk, talk, talk

If an **I** is awake, they're probably talking. They *love* to talk. I's are very extroverted in nature (big surprise, I know). Because they tend to have loud voices, you'll never have to wonder what they're talking about—you'll hear them loud and clear. In fact, even their whisper is loud.

They also often talk with their hands. I'm convinced that their mouths are somehow connected to their hands. I believe that if you were to hold their hands still, they wouldn't be able to talk.

Event of the day...every day

At my house, we usually have an "event of the day." **I**'s can turn any simple task or excursion into a huge ordeal. If you're married to an **I**, you know exactly what I'm talking about. Between my high **I** daughter and my **I** husband, there's always something happening.

Either my husband has left something at home he needs for work, or has fallen through the attic (again), or some other crisis or event has occurred. I'll never forget a trip that my husband and I took several years ago. I was flying in to Atlanta from a location other than home, and he was flying in from home. We were going to meet up in Atlanta and continue on to California, where I had a speaking engagement. It was going to be a great weekend get-away, as well as an opportunity to catch up with some high school friends of his that lived there.

Because I didn't have my laptop and projector with me at the time, my husband was going to bring them with him from our house. I was very worried that he was going to forget them. If he did, I would be in big trouble. On my way to the airport, I thought, "As long as he remembers my laptop and projector, everything will be okay and we'll have time to enjoy a nice breakfast together at the airport before hopping on the next flight." That was my vision. Unfortunately, it didn't happen that way.

My husband's flight was very early that morning. Sadly, the night before, he found out that the father of one of his friends had passed away several months before. Since my husband is part **S**, he's very sentimental in nature. He stayed awake most of the night reflecting on what a wonderful man this person was. He thought about all the great times. He mourned for his friend. He didn't get much sleep as you can imagine. In fact, since he went to bed so late, he woke up late the next morning.

He rushes to the airport like a mad man. On the way, he calls me to let me know he's late. He had trouble getting his backpack to zip up because of the video recorder and camera bag he stuffed into it. He gets to the airport, pulls right up to the curb, jumps out, gets his ticket at curbside check in, and then drives to the lot where he normally parks. It's closed. He cruises around trying to find the cheapest place to park. He finally finds a place, then hops on the shuttle back to the airport. When he gets to the airport, he can't find his ticket. He left it in the car. He takes the shuttle back to the parking garage, grabs his ticket, and then back to the airport he goes.

At airport security, my husband is the lucky winner. He is chosen to be strip-searched (well, not entirely, but heck, close enough). They scatter his belongings in the process. Once he's given the nod, he quickly shoves everything back into his bag, runs to the gate, and barely makes the plane.

All is well, right? Please, let me continue. When he gets off the plane in Atlanta, I'm waiting at the gate. I notice that he has my laptop and projector. I am thinking, "Thank you, God." I also notice, however, that his backpack looks a little empty. It certainly wasn't full enough to be difficult to zip up. I say to him, "I thought you had trouble zipping up your backpack." He looks at the backpack. "Yeah," he agrees, "I was wondering why it didn't feel as heavy." He opens the backpack and, you guessed it, no video recorder and camera bag. "Maybe I left it on our bed at home," he says. So, we call our neighbors at 6 a.m. and ask them to break into our house and check to see if it's there. No luck.

"Maybe I left it at the security line," he guesses again. So, we call TSA (Transportation Safety Administration) and ask them to check the security line. Nothing. "Maybe I left it in the car," he says. So, we call the parking garage company and have them check the car. The bag is there.

You probably deduced that we did not get the relaxing breakfast I had envisioned. In fact, we barely made our connection.

Of course, as a **D**, I made sure to remind him about the missing video recorder/camera bag during the entire trip. Everything we saw that would've been nice to get a picture of, I would say something like, "Gee, wouldn't it have been nice to take a picture of that? Wow, too bad we don't have a camera with us." Evil, I know.

On another occasion, I was traveling to an event as a guest speaker. When my plane landed, I called home to tell my husband I had made it safely. I could tell by the tone in his voice that the "event of the day" had occurred. I asked him what was wrong and he replied, "I lost my wedding ring." Now as a high **D**-type, I try to live by "It is what it is." In my mind, this was disappointing, but my thought was, the ring could be replaced. In his mind, since he is also a high **S** personality, this was a sentimental object from our wedding day. It was engraved inside and had a cross etched in it that matched my wedding ring. He was devastated that he couldn't find it. In fact, he spent all afternoon looking for it. He had taken the kids to his workplace to look. He even checked the sink in every bathroom. Not there. He retraced his steps as best he could. Nothing.

I told him I was very sorry to hear about his ring and that I would call him when I got to the hotel. When I called him the second time, he exclaimed, "I found my ring!" I replied, "Great! Where was it?" He said, "In the baby's pants." What? Evidently, the ring had slipped off his finger when he was changing the baby. The ring was looser than usual because he had recently lost weight. (For the record, I told him he should have his ring re-sized; he clearly didn't listen to me.)

As a **D**, it was very amusing to me that the ring was actually with him everywhere he looked for it. He was toting it around in the baby's pants the entire time. Isn't that hilarious? I think so.

My daughter is no different. Just yesterday, we were at a major retail store that starts with a big red "T" and has a logo that looks like a bull's-eye (hey, I don't want to chance getting sued if I actually say their name). We left the store and drove to a restaurant for lunch. As soon as I got the two younger kids out of the car, my daughter says, "Where is my purse? Oh, no! I think I left it in the shopping cart at the store." Sigh.

I immediately load the kids back into the car and drive back to the store. My two younger kids cry the entire way because they're hungry. My daughter panics the entire way because she thinks her purse is gone forever. I'm trying to convince myself the entire way that none of this will matter in ten years. Luckily, the purse was still in the shopping cart. Tragedy avoided.

Messy is fun

Speaking of my eldest daughter, when it comes to cleaning her room and keeping her stuff organized, she's definitely an **I**. They could care less about orderly closets and neatly folded clothes. If the drawer shuts, that's good enough. To them, the joy of discovery is half the fun. They may reach into the drawer and pull something out that they haven't seen for a while and happily exclaim, "Hey, I forgot I had that!" It's new all over again.

And when you tell an **I** to clean their room, they go into the room and shove everything under the bed. They look around with delight and say to themselves, "There. Room's clean."

The quintessential salesperson

The **I** personality usually dominates in sales. They're quick on their feet and make contacts very easily. Going after business is what they do best. And since they have no idea when people are trying to get away, they just keep talking. Have you ever wondered if someone gives in to an **I** just to make them stop talking? I do this with my husband at times.

Where were we going, again?

Remember how I described how a **D** stands on a street corner? How an **I** stands on the street corner is very different. They would be window shopping or talking with friends. They might, in fact, completely forget where they're going in the first place and decide to go shopping instead. After all, they saw something pretty in the window that's on sale. It's that shiny object thing.

All is forgiven because...I forgot

If you upset an **I**, don't worry— they don't hold grudges. Why? Because the next day they can't remember who said the mean thing any way. As a

D, I wish I had this quality. Unfortunately, a **D** can go to bed angry and wake up angrier. With **I**'s, it's a brand new day. How wonderful!

I's also live for the moment for the exact same reason. Long-term memory for an **I** is a challenge, so they tend to forget quickly what happened yesterday. In some ways, this is great, but in other ways, not so much.

You're late! Again.

The secret to success is to never tell an **I** what time you really need to be somewhere. Always give them a much earlier time.

Earlier in the book, I mentioned one particular personality that is always late. The mystery is now solved…it's the **I**. They have absolutely no concept of time.

Since my husband is part **I**, lateness is almost a daily ritual in my life. As such, I get lots of practice living by my two rules: "It is what it is," and "Will it matter in ten years?" If I didn't recite these rules regularly, I can tell you, I would be walking around annoyed and frustrated—a lot.

Starters

"Go!" says this personality. They're great at starting stuff. If you need something started, go find an **I**. They will get the ball rolling. We'll talk about the finishing stuff part later…

Idea people

I's often exclaim, "I have a great idea!" They're extremely creative and adept at coming up with new and exciting projects. They excel at dreaming up themes for parties, decorating schemes, or anything else that uses their creativity.

Then they charm other people into doing the "work" part of the idea. Can you do that? You can if you are an **I**.

Everybody's their friend

None of the other personalities can make friends as easily as an **I**. **I**'s will talk to pretty much everyone: the person in the taxi cab, the elevator, the grocery line—anywhere. And, after a five-minute conversation, they're introducing this person to others as their new friend. No wonder they're so good in sales.

Storytellers

I-types take twice as long to tell a story than it should take any human being to tell a story. And the more response they receive from the listener, the better the story.

> I always suggest taking what an I says with a grain of salt. Believe, but verify, is a good approach.

Some people become jealous because all of the exciting things seem to happen to the **I**'s. Well, here's their secret—they make it up. To them, a story is not about being factual, it's about entertainment. To them, there's nothing wrong with "fluffing it up a bit." Needless to say, they're very imaginative.

Speaking without knowing

Have you ever met someone who can talk about anything, no matter what the topic? That person is most likely an **I**. **I**'s can talk about absolutely any subject—with or without information. They will say whatever comes to mind, whether it makes sense or not. This drives **C**'s crazy.

I don't need a stinking plan

Routine? Perfectionism? These words are unfamiliar to an **I**-type. They prefer to go with whatever strikes them at the moment. No need to plan anything—just go with the flow. **I**'s think perfection is boring. They think, "I'd rather spend my time having fun than trying to be perfect."

They also don't expect anyone else to be perfect. They have low expectations of themselves and low expectations of others. They believe people should just be able to do whatever they want, and no one should care.

Try it, you'll like it

It's never been done before? That doesn't stop an **I**. **I**'s enjoy new experiences and trying things that no one else has ever tried. They aren't intimidated by this. They think, "What's the worst that could happen?"

I is for inspiration

"Inspiration" is a wonderful word to describe an **I**. **I**'s offer a lot to the world. They're great at persuading and motivating others. They're captivating and good at drawing others in to whatever they're doing.

Their energy tends to attract and inspire those around them. If you find yourself lacking energy, just go find an **I** to rub off on you. They're full of it (energy that is)!

Do you know an **I**? I hope so. Everyone needs to have one in their life. In the next chapter, I'll talk about some potential pitfalls for the **I**-type.

CHAPTER 6

The Challenging Side of I

Are you starting to recall a few **I**'s that you know? As you can see, there are many great things about being an **I**. Personally, I quite enjoy it. Unfortunately, there are some that are annoyed by our **I**-ness. They think **I**'s are flaky, untruthful, egotistical, messy, unreliable, irrational, impulsive, illogical people that talk way too much. A bit judgmental, I agree.

Again, just because others think this doesn't mean you necessarily *are* any of these things. But, the truth is, if you are a high **I**, you probably possess one or two of these pitfalls. As I said earlier, personalities are different depending upon whether they're under control or out of control.

If you are a high **I**, decide which of the two words apply to you in each column. Be honest.

Under Control	Out Of Control
Optimistic	Unrealistic
Persuasive	Manipulative
Excited	Emotional
Communicative	Gossip
Spontaneous	Impulsive
Outgoing	Unfocused
Expressive	Excitable
Involved	Directionless
Imaginative	Day dreamer
Warm and friendly	Purposeless

There are two major things that keep this personality type from making necessary changes:

- They seldom follow through
- They don't believe they have any major faults

I-types also tend to:

- Speak very quickly
- Have trouble saying "no" to others
- Say whatever comes to mind, without thinking about how it might affect others
- Be casual in meeting deadlines
- Answer questions asked of other people
- Run late
- Dominate conversations
- Forget about appointments

Humiliate me and you'll regret it

If you ever publicly embarrass an **I**, you'll know it and regret it. They don't tolerate being humiliated in front of others. They will turn on you in a heartbeat if they feel like you are putting them down.

If you are an **I**, work on keeping criticism to yourself. Do not attack the person who embarrassed you until it's the appropriate time. Then, talk calmly to that person about how they made you feel.

Would you please let me finish what I was saying?

I's often know what they're going to say before the other person has even stopped talking. If you are an **I**, you have probably caught yourself talking over someone else. You also tend not to hear what the other person is saying to you. You are too excited about your turn to talk. You are also trying really hard not to forget what you want to say.

Practice being sensitive to the interests of others and learn to listen.

Forget me not

Have you ever seen someone in the parking lot of a large store and he or she is wandering around trying to set off their car alarm? That person is probably an **I**. They forgot where they parked. If they own more than one car, they may not even remember which car they drove.

If you ever lend something to an **I**, make sure you get it back. They may forget who lent it to them in the first place and never return it. After a while, they may assume they have always had it, or that they bought it. This is not intentional; they're just forgetful by nature.

Liar, liar, pants on fire

Often times, other personalities view **I**'s as untruthful. It's hard for **I**'s to understand why they may be perceived that way. Let me explain.

First, **I**'s typically make decisions using emotion instead of logic. If one person asks an **I** how they feel about something, the **I** will tell them how they feel *right that minute*. The **I** may feel completely differently just a few hours later, however. So, if a second person asks how they feel about the same thing, they will very likely get a different answer. Inevitably, these two people will get together and think the **I** is talking out of both sides of his or her mouth.

Second, **I**'s are great at volunteering for jobs. Unfortunately, they forget they committed to doing it. This causes other personality types to say, "Don't ask them to do it. They will *say* that they will do it, but it will never get done."

I also mentioned in the last chapter that **I**'s are the best storytellers on earth. Unfortunately, most of their stories are made up. They are master exaggerators. **I**'s see no harm "puffing up" a story a bit as long as everyone is having a great time. They also feel that people may not like them if they aren't exciting.

I's, you need to be careful about telling a story for the effect, not the truth. If someone doesn't understand this about you, they may be disappointed when they find out a story was only half true. Unfortunately, this can cause people not to trust you. And believe me, you are an exciting enough person without having to exaggerate. Just be you and people will love you for it.

If you're a parent, it's important to understand that if you have an **I** child, they're probably lying to you left, right, up, down, and diagonally. Why? Because they want life to be about having fun, not about being accountable. If you do not address this early on, it can follow them into adulthood and become a natural way for them to live.

We all have met a compulsive liar at some point in our lives. That person probably started out as an **I**. Give your child a personality assessment so you know what their strengths are, what their challenges are, and where they go under pressure. It will also give you guidance to raise them the way they need to be raised based on their personalities.

You can purchase assessments for children by going to my Web site at **www.personalityprofiles.org** and clicking on "Order Materials." There are several different assessments to choose from. I recommend the 48-page assessment because there is a section in there that shows how your child learns. This is valuable information to share with their teachers. Your child doesn't need to know how to read, by the way; he or she just needs to be at least four years old.

Finish what you start

In the last chapter, I mentioned that **I**'s are great starters. Well, unfortunately, they're not great finishers. As soon as a project becomes boring, or feels too much like "work," they're not interested in finishing it. They have tons of unfinished stuff in their lives.

I's, try to be a good finishers, and not just a good starters. Give yourself a little reward for each step that you finish in the project to motivate yourself to complete it. You can do it. Do it now!

Are you talking too much?

I's tend to talk too much. If you are an **I**, try talking half as much as you normally do. Look for signs of boredom in others. Seriously, if people's eyes are glazing over, or they are walking away from you, then it's probably time to condense your comments—not follow them out of the room. Try to have some SA (situational awareness).

Living in the moment

Because **I**-types are easily influenced, they must be careful about living in the moment. Often they don't think about the consequences, they think only about whatever they're getting at the moment.

This attitude is very dangerous. Remember, the pleasure of the moment never exceeds the pain of the memory. Maybe you have lied to someone to get what you want. Maybe you have been unfaithful to a spouse to have pleasure for the moment. This is never the right decision. Try to look down the road at the consequences of your actions instead of just living for the moment. Realize that most of your decisions don't affect just you. Think about others you are affecting and ask yourself if it's worth it.

Clutter control

I's are typically very disorganized. They do try from time to time. They really want to improve. They think, "I'm going to clean out my car and, this time, it's going to stay clean." About a week later, if not less, the car is in the same messy state as before.

Being a high **I**, my husband implements a specific process that helps him tremendously with clutter control. Every time he gets home, he empties out his car right away—even if we arrive home at 2 a.m. after a long trip.

If you are an **I**, this might be a great process for you, too. (Feel free to thank my hubby if it works.)

Keep track of my money? No way.

Do you balance your checkbook? If you do, you are not an **I**. **I**'s think, "If I have checks, I must have money." And, if they bother to note the amount of each check they write, they round the number up. For example, if they spend $13.68 they write down $14.00. This helps them because they work better with even numbers. Luckily, with today's technology, they can count on the bank to track everything for them electronically—a lifesaver for **I**'s.

Directionally challenged

Where is north, south, east, or west? Don't ask an **I** because they probably don't know. When they give directions, they use landmarks. They're very visual in nature. They may say something like, "Go to Walmart and turn left. Then go to the ice cream shop and turn right."

I's are also not good at listening to directions.

Work? I'll do that later

If an **I** perceives something as work, they're not interested in doing it. They're "people" people, not "task" people. When it comes to doing something they consider work (mowing the lawn, cleaning the house, taking out the trash) they delay it for as long as possible—or get someone else to do it for them.

Colors, not numbers

It's very difficult for an **I**-type to remember names, dates, and facts. They function better by remembering color. I always encourage this personality type to incorporate color into their lives as much as possible.

I-type children and ADHD

Although this book is not about parenting, there is something very important I want you to know: many **I**-type children are misdiagnosed with ADHD (Attention-Deficit Hyperactivity Disorder).

Why? Let's think about teachers for a moment. Teachers are mostly one of two personalities—usually an **S** or a **C**. Both of these personality types believe students should sit down, be quiet, follow directions, and pay attention. This is does not work for an **I**-type child.

An **I** child doesn't hear the teacher say that there is a test tomorrow because they were busy watching a butterfly in the corner do some pretty cool tricks. On their way home from the bus, they drop half of their homework papers on the side of the road. Eventually the teacher calls the parents and says, "Something is wrong with your child."

Because you don't know any better, you take your child to a psychologist. Guess what personality psychologists are? Usually **C**'s. After speaking with your child for five minutes, they agree that something is wrong and write you a prescription for some type of medication.

You may be asking how I know this. Through direct experience. When my eldest child was about ten years old, I took her to a psychologist to see what they would say. I knew she was a high **I**, so I knew why she had particular challenges in school. The doctor talked to my child for, literally, 30 seconds and I walked out with a prescription for Ridilin. Thirty seconds. Seriously? I can tell you that to diagnose ADHD correctly, the process takes much longer than that. There are blood tests and other processes involved. Many other disorders, by the way, are commonly misdiagnosed as ADHD, so be careful.

Now, there are definitely children that need medication. Unfortunately, we live in a medicated society. If you suspect that your child has ADHD, please make sure that they're assessed properly. And I urge you, *never* walk into a doctor's office and walk out the same day with a prescription.

A friend of mine who spent many years in the school system told me that someone did a study and found that there is a 97 percent ADHD misdiagnosis error rate. Please, keep your child from being a statistic. It's so important that we understand the personalities of our children. Give them a personality assessment instead of a pill.

I affirmations

Here are some great affirmations for I's that will, subconsciously, help you improve your challenges. Write them down three times each when you start your day. Remember to add some of your own to the list.

- I am an excellent finisher.
- I communicate openly and honestly with everyone I talk to.

- I enjoy doing tasks and getting things done.
- I make my own decisions without letting others influence me negatively.
- I listen intently when people are talking to me.
- I work efficiently and love to see the results.
- I make logical, well thought-out decisions.

I's, you are wonderful people. I hope you realize all the great things you have to offer. Enjoy being **I**nspiring!

CHAPTER 7

Getting to Know the Supportive S

S personalities make the world a better place just by existing. S-types are the hardest of all personalities to spot. They don't exhibit any obvious traits like other personalities. Sometimes you have to figure them out by process of elimination. If they're not moving, jumping, waving, and wiggling, you know they're not a **D** or an **I**. S-types:

- Are the easiest of all the personalities to get along with
- Are the closest there is to being a balanced person
- Make good mediators
- Can be happy anywhere
- Are steady and low key
- Pride themselves on not letting people know how they feel

The **S**-type life motto is: "It really doesn't matter that much." They don't understand why other personalities get so upset about things. Wouldn't it be nice if we all had this **S** trait?

> Because this personality is so very mild mannered and sweet, I can't bring myself to mess with an **S** like I can other personalities.

S-types are the good guys. They would rather listen and support than be center stage. They don't need to be in the spot light. They just want to help others, even if they never receive recognition.

If it ain't broke, don't replace it

Remember how I said that once luggage with wheels was invented, some personality types immediately threw out their old luggage and bought the new, improved version? The **S**-type is probably not one of them. You'll see them at the airport still carrying their old-fashioned, beat up suitcases. They think, "It still works. And as long as it works, I am going to keep using it. When it breaks I will get another one." This is also the same mindset of the **C** personality. (We'll get to them next.)

I remember when my husband, an **S/I** blend, and I got married. He still had the one and only car he bought when he finished college. When we met, there were over 100,000 miles on it. I know there are many cars that are still dependable with that many miles, but this wasn't one of them.

During one of our military moves, I had to sit with my legs to one side in the front seat because it was raining and water was dripping from the outside of the car and onto my feet. There was also an electrical shortage in the visor, which caused the battery to drain. It also didn't let you know when you were low on gas. I can't tell you how many times I held my breath and prayed we made it to the next gas station (since my husband is an **I** he often didn't notice we were low on gas until we were running on fumes). It also squeaked as if there were a bunch of mice inside the engine running on a wheel to make the car operate. I wouldn't be surprised if there were. We spent more money repairing the car than the car was worth.

And although I rarely drove his car because it was so unreliable, it still annoyed me that I had to pick him up every time it broke down. Even with all its assorted problems, my husband still loved that car. To him, it functioned well enough and, until it completely stopped running, he was going to cling to it like a security blanket. Only an **S** or **C** would think like this.

One of the best days of my life was when that car finally died—as in, never coming back to life. I took pictures of the wrecker hauling it away.

You said what?

S-types are so helpful, almost to a fault. Sometimes their "helpfulness" can get them into trouble. Here's a situation that occurred between one of my **D** friends and her **S** husband.

My friend was frustrated about her weight and wanted to lose 20 pounds—now! She told her husband she was going upstairs to call a personal trainer she had used in the past. When she reached the top of the stairs, her husband, who was at the bottom of the stairs said, "Really, sweetheart, I think you only need to lose about 15 pounds."

Her kind hubby now has a scar on his forehead from the high heel my friend took off and zinged at him like a bullet out of a shotgun. Sometimes love hurts.

Light of foot

Unlike **D**'s, who you know when there is one in the office, **S**-types are light footed and can pass by without a whisper. They may have been in the office for hours, but you never knew it. This personality has a way of coming into a room and quietly moving around unnoticed, so you are surprised to find out they've been there for a while.

Street corner sweet

When you see an **S** on a busy street corner, they will act differently than the **D**'s and **I**'s we discussed previously. They will make pleasant conversation with people around them, tell them to have a nice day, and let the person go in front of them.

What should I order…?

If an **S** is ordering food at a restaurant, it may take them a while. They have trouble making decisions. In fact, if you've ever had someone ask you to order for them, it was probably an **S**.

While **D** and **I** types prefer lots of choices, the **S**-type prefers limited choices. After all, lots of choices means more decisions— and making a decision is hard for them. It can become even more overwhelming. We'll talk more about their decision-making challenge in the next chapter.

Emotional rescuers

S-types laugh with those who laugh and cry with those who cry. They're emotionally involved in whatever is going on around them. They also have an inner desire to rescue people and animals from their troubles. The **S** is the personality type who starts animal rescue shelters.

Friends galore

The S-type is the most sentimental of all the personalities. They save old yearbooks, love notes, and poems, and place high value on friendship and stability. My husband has many friends from childhood who he keeps in contact with, which is challenging when you are in the military and always moving. But he works hard to do so because friendships are so important to him.

Will join in if invited

S-types are socially reserved. Isn't that an oxymoron? They enter a room slowly with a half smile. If there is a chair in the room, they may head straight for it.

They do, however, love being included in conversations, but won't force their way in. Instead, they linger around the outside of conversational groups listening in, but don't join in unless invited.

This is the polar opposite of D's who step into the middle of a crowd and say, "What are you talking about?"

I don't care

"I don't care. What do *you* want to do?" is said a lot by the S-type. This is to prevent rocking the boat or causing trouble, or having to make yet another decision. And, as opposed to D's, S-types really mean it.

For example, when you ask a D where they want to eat, they may say, "I don't care, where do you want to go?" But if you pick a place the D doesn't like they will tell you pronto. It's as if they're saying, "I gave you a chance, but you blew it." Instead, they'll respond with a short, "No, we're not going there. I want to go here."

Team players

If you want a real team player, just find an **S**. They cooperate well with others. In fact, they seek acceptance and teamwork. This is very different from the **D**-type; **D**'s only wants to be on a team if *they're* in charge of it.

Change is bad

S-types are more comfortable with the known and expected. They're not interested in change; they're happy with the way things are. Comfort, safety, and security are very important to them.

Impatient and insensitive people beware

This personality type has a high degree of patience and sensitivity— so much so, that they're very annoyed by people who *are* impatient or insensitive. If you want to see an **S** act like a **D**, just expose them to one or two of those attitudes. It's one of the few times you'll see them angry.

> S-types dislike conflict so much, that they have the ability to blend in with their environment to avoid it.

Clamming up on conflict

Have you ever tried to fight with this personality? You won't get far. **S**-types dislike and avoid conflict. In fact, sometimes if you are trying to argue with an **S**, they just stop talking. This really annoys **D**'s because when **D**'s yell they expect others to yell back. When an **S** refuses to yell back, the **D** gets even angrier.

Middle of the road

Unlike **I**'s, the **S** personality does not participate in extremes. They stay solidly in the middle of the road. To other types, they may appear to be too laid back or blasé about things. If you are not an **S**-type, this is hard for you to imagine because things that you find important or would get upset over, this type does not.

Quality over quantity

If you are looking for quality work, an **S** can provide it. They're much more interested in quality than quantity. Unlike **D**'s and **I**'s, with their "good enough" attitudes, the **S**-types will perform to the best of their ability. (**C**-types also possess this trait.)

Know a lot about a little

An **S** prefers to have an area of specialization. Where some personalities prefer to know a little about many things, the **S** wants to know a lot about a few subjects. If you are not careful, you may be fooled and think they're a **D** when you see them in an environment where they're very comfortable, confident, and competent.

Blue jeans and sweatshirt people

S-types dress differently and more conservatively than **D** and **I** types. They love jeans and sweatshirts or more casual and comfortable clothing.

More on S-types

S-types are also often:

- Witty with a dry, subtle sense of humor

- Loyal

- Detail-oriented, methodical, and systematic

- Want high touch, not high tech

- Respond best to warmth and friendliness

- Do not care about status and prestige

- Enjoy using checklists and taking notes (not to be confused with C's, who also do this)

As you can see, there are so many great things about S-types. As I mentioned, my husband is an **S/I** blend, and I have learned so much from him. We are constantly receiving products or services from businesses just because we took the time to actually care about people and go out of our way to be friendly. I would've never done this naturally, but I learned it from my sweet **S** husband. Thank you, dear! That little tip was definitely worth my time to learn.

In the next chapter, I'll talk about the few places an **S** might have some challenges.

☆ CHAPTER 8 ☆

The Challenging Side of S

Personally, I love the **S**-type so much that I married one! Unfortunately, there are those that may get annoyed by **S** traits. Some people think **S**-types are lazy, slow, boring, stubborn, unconfident, overly sensitive, weak, indecisive, and repetitive. Too bad for them.

Sorry to disappoint all you **S**-types out there, but you don't get to escape doing your self assessment. You, like all of the other personality types, have traits that can be under control and out of control.

Take a look at the list on the next page and choose the word from each column that applies to you most. Remember, you are still a great person and we love you very much. Do not take this personally. This is just to help you notice one or two pitfalls.

Under Control	Out of Control
Relaxed	Lacking initiative
Reliable	Dependent
Cooperative	A sucker
Stable	Indecisive
Good listener	Uncommunicative
Single-minded	Inflexible
Steadfast	Resistant to change
Softhearted	Easily manipulated
Systematic	Slow
Amiable	Resentful

I'm no fool

S-types are often worried about making fools of themselves. This keeps them from participating in things that other personalities don't think twice about.

For example, years ago, my husband, Dennis, and I were looking to buy a home in Alabama at a time when the market was hot and homes were selling quickly. One evening, at about 8:30 p.m., I was searching the local MLS (multiple listing service), a Web site that shows all homes currently available for sale. I noticed a home in the neighborhood I wanted to live in that had just gone on the market. I also noticed that it was on the same street that our preacher lived on. I asked my husband, "Do you know where the preacher lives?" He confirmed that he did. I said, "Great. Let's go over right now. I want to find out if he's seen the inside of this house." Because if he has, I was thinking, he may know what the floor plan is like, why they're selling, and if they're motivated. As a **D**, I need to know it all—now.

Because my husband is an **S**, he agreed. So, we hopped in the car, drove to the street, and pulled into a driveway. As I started to get out of the car, a conversation ensued as follows.

Dennis:	Wait!
Me:	What? Let's go.
Dennis:	I'm not sure if this is the house.
Me:	What do you mean you're not sure if this is the house? You said you know where the preacher lives."
Dennis:	Well, I'm not sure if it's this house or the one next door.
Me:	Well, go to the door and ask.
Dennis:	No way!

You see, I asked my husband to do more than an **S** is capable of doing. He was not going to make a fool of himself by knocking on the wrong door at 8:30 at night.

But as a **D**, I don't intend to give up (again, because of my need to know everything *now*). So, I started assessing our surroundings. I thought, "The preacher has four kids. The garage is full of bikes, there's a basketball goal in the driveway, and a Jesus fish on the back of a truck. I'm going in." So, I got out of the car and knocked on the door. Sure enough, it was the preacher's house.

As a **D**, this did not take me outside my comfort zone at all, but for an **S**, this is nearly impossible to do. (For the record, we did not buy the house. Some personalities want to know the rest of the story, so there you go.)

Decisions, decisions

Yes, no, yes, no…maybe. If you know people who have trouble making decisions, they're probably **S**-types. Decisions are a daily challenge for them. And I'm not talking life changing decisions, I mean any decision—even the most trivial. Something that is so simple to the other personalities is often a trial for an **S**.

Years ago, when I was taking a nap, my husband woke me up. Waking up a **D** is not a good idea, unless the house is on fire or some other life-threatening emergency is happening. But waking a **D** up to ask her if she thought he should eat first or exercise first is a bad, bad thing. Scary, really.

Another time, our daughter asked my husband for ten dollars. He had one ten dollar bill in one hand and one five dollar bill and five one dollars bills in his other hand. He took, literally, five solid minutes—which, believe me, seemed wayyyyyy longer—to decide which to give her. He looked back and forth, back and forth, glancing at one hand and then the other saying things like, "Hmm, which one should I give her?" and "She might need some ones, but then I might also need some ones." Oh. My. Stars. As a **D**-type, I lost all patience and almost screamed. I said, "It doesn't matter! It's ten dollars either way. If she needs ones, she'll get them. If you need ones, you'll get them!"

Just last week, my husband and I attended an Atlanta Braves baseball game. It was Memorial Day and the squadron he commands was going to put the American flag on the field at the start of the game. After the flag ceremony, as we were headed to our seats, one of the marketing people for the Braves asked my husband to participate in their version of "Wheel of Fortune" during one of the breaks. My **S** husband agreed to help them out.

When he played the game, he answered very quickly because he already knew the answer based on the clue they had given. When he got back to his seat, he asked me, "Do you think I should have taken longer to answer instead of saying the answer right away? Do you think that other people who were watching believe that they must have told me the answer since I said it so quickly? What do you think I should have done?" I'm thinking, "Are you kidding me? Do you really think anyone in the audience is sitting around thinking that you should have taken longer to answer the question?" Because I love my husband though, I simply replied, "You did a great job!"

Here's another one. About a year ago, I observed a teenage girl at an ice cream shop. She couldn't decide what to order. She asked everyone's opinion in her group. She let other people go in front of her for at least ten minutes. Finally, she ordered but questioned her decision afterward—definitely an **S**.

Another time, I was conducting a seminar for a room full of teens. An **S** in the room told me a story about he and his friend—also an **S**—going to a movie. When they got to the theater, the movie was sold out. They proceeded to sit in the car for *two hours* deciding what to do next. As a **D**, I was inwardly cringing as he told me this. I was thinking, "You just wasted two hours! Why didn't you just go to another movie?" When I asked him how he felt about it, he responded, "It was great! We had fun just spending time together." Can you imagine sitting around not making a decision being fun? *Only* if you are a high **S**.

S is for stubborn

Here's the funny thing about **S**-types…once they do make up their minds, they aren't changing them. They figure, "It took me long enough to make this stupid decision in the first place. If I change my mind, I'll have to start all over again." So, they stick with their decision—even if they find out it wasn't such a good one.

Sucker!

S-types sometimes put themselves in a position of being a sucker. Others may easily take advantage of you if they see you as an easy target. Unfortunately, your kind heart can get you burned and burn you out. Understand that you can't be all things to all people. Practice making decisions and learn to say, "No."

Express yourself

> Learn to express your feelings and not just have a quiet will of iron.

S-types avoid conflict like the plague. In fact, they're often way too concerned about conflict.

Don't be afraid to address things that need addressing. You are sweet, so will probably find a non-confrontational way to approach the issue anyway.

Tepid responders

S-types are often married to D's or I's. And often, D's and I's come home excited about some wonderful idea or plan they cooked up. They explain it enthusiastically to their S spouse, only to get a very lukewarm, "That sounds good, honey." The D or I then thinks, "Wow, your thrilled response is overwhelming. I should sit down or I may faint."

S-types, you must to learn to get excited and show enthusiasm, or others will feel like what is important to them doesn't matter to you. (Although keep in mind that if an **I**-type is telling you their idea, they don't necessarily have any intention of actually doing it—they just want to talk about how fun it *would* be. Tomorrow they may be excited about something completely different.)

Excuses, Excuses

S-types are so loving and forgiving that that these qualities may become a weakness. They tend to want to give others one chance after the other. They often try to explain away someone's poor decisions. Unfortunately, by doing so, they enable the person to continually make bad decisions.

For example, recently two 17-year-olds were killed, tragically, in a car accident in the town I live in. Both of them had issues with previous wrecks, drinking and driving, and so on. In fact, the parents of one of the teens tried to hire an attorney a year earlier, to defend their son against a DUI. When the attorney voiced his disgust about the parents defending the boy's deplorable actions, they chose not to hire him. A year later, their son is dead, just days before he finished his junior year of high school.

Are *you* an enabler? Be careful not to let your traits of forgiveness and understanding turn into an enabling weakness. You could be causing more harm than good.

Taking care of you

> Learn to express your feelings and not just have a quiet will of iron.

S-types can be such sacrificial givers, which is a great trait, but they must remember that they deserve to be treated as well as everyone else.

Recently, I was talking to an S who had just lost her job due to some medical challenges that prevented her from working. She had worked for her company for several years and was very dedicated. She didn't feel like she should file for disability.

When I asked her what advice she would give to someone else in the same situation, she replied, "I would tell them to take the disability." I then asked her why she doesn't do the same, and she replied, "Because I'm not worthy." How sad.

A changing world

Another big challenge for S-types is adapting to change. They want everything to stay the same—always. They want to drive the same car, use the same VCR (please!), the same computer and software, and so on.

The world is constantly changing. Most jobs require you to adapt. In fact, if you tried to do business the same way it was done ten years ago, you'd be out of business quick as a wink. For example, if you own a payroll company and insist on doing all the books manually instead of using a computer program, most companies aren't going to give you their business.

My husband demonstrates this challenge when he needs to replace things. For example, he loses his sunglasses frequently because he is part **I** so has to replace them. He purchased his first pair of the brand and style he wears on our honeymoon, so each time he loses them, he buys the exact same kind because the **S** side of him is sentimental. This means ordering about ten pairs of sunglasses from Mexico each year. Mucho dinero.

He also has to have the exact same deodorant, shampoo, toothpaste, and so on. When his watch breaks, we have to search long and hard to find the same exact kind. This becomes a challenge after about ten years or so.

No go on the status quo

S-types are so comfortable with the known, that it sometimes prevents them from having high goals or great expectations. They're often slow to take the initiative, particularly in the work environment.

> Remember, you are born to be excellent, so don't condition yourself to be mediocre!

They're very dependable and will do everything their boss asks of them, but when they have completed all required work, usually they will not start doing other things on their own. They're afraid the boss will get upset since they weren't asked to do that yet. Or, maybe they'd do it differently than the boss wants. So instead, they sit there and do nothing.

Try to step outside of your comfort zone. Set goals and work hard to meet them instead of just accepting the status quo.

Fighting the perception of laziness

If **S**-types aren't careful, they can be perceived as lazy by other personalities—particularly if they announce that they're going to do a task.

Anytime an **S** has a choice between being with people or accomplishing a task, they usually choose to be with people. This can be a challenge if there are personalities around that want those tasks done.

One time my husband said, "Tomorrow, I'm going to get up and file all the papers piled on top of the file cabinet." My response was, "Great! That really needs to be done." The next morning when we got up, here's how it went down:

Dennis:	Hey, do you want to go out and get some breakfast?
Me:	I thought you wanted to file all the papers on top of the filing cabinet.
Dennis:	Yeah, but I can do that later. I'd rather spend time with the family.

S-types must practice not putting off until tomorrow what they can do today.

Monotaskers

D's and **I**'s love to multitask; **S**-types and **C**'s do not. They prefer to work on one or two things at a time. They get flustered with too many priorities. This is especially challenging when an **S**-type marries a **D** or **I**. The lifestyle of these multitasking personalities drives **S**-types and **C**'s around the bend. They literally feel like they're being run over.

Procrastinators

Although **S**-types are great finishers, they have trouble actually starting. They're so people-oriented that they often delay tasks for as long as possible. Unfortunately, they sometimes put themselves under the absolute most pressure they can stand before starting the project. If a project is due on Tuesday, they may not start it until Monday night. They will stay up all night to complete it. Talk about stress!

Thin skins

S-types take everything personally. Unfortunately, they dwell on things that other personalities don't even think about. They need to practice having thicker skin and not taking everything to heart. I'll talk more about how to help with this in a later chapter.

S affirmations

Affirmations for **S**-types include:
- I am confident and communicate effectively.
- I make quick decisions.
- I love accomplishing tasks and being a quick starter.
- I am an excellent multitasker.
- I love to take care of myself and do nice things for me.

If you write these down three times each at the beginning of your day, you'll be off to a great start.

You are really appreciated, **S**-types. I hope you learned some great stuff about yourself that will help you to have better relationships with those that are important to you. Thank you for caring so much about others. You are the ones that fill this world with love and compassion. You have hearts of gold.

CHAPTER 9

Getting to Know the Cautious C

hat would the world do without the cautious **C**? They keep all the rest of us straight and out of trouble. **C**'s tend to:

- Be more introverted in nature
- Prefer to work alone
- Be deep thinkers
- Be quiet and thoughtful
- Be good strategists

Sound like anyone you know? I hope so. We all need at least one **C**-type in our lives. This personality is more formal and proper than other types, but they're the most reliable. If they tell you they're going to do something, you don't have to worry about it—they'll get it done, and they'll get it done right. **C**'s think that if it's worth doing, it should be done correctly. Otherwise, why spend time, money, and effort on it?

Minutiae is beautiful

C's are very competent. They know that they know what they know. And they love to learn—four levels deep—about any topic. They love

> C's see things in black and white, and not much grey. It's either wrong or right, period.

computers and other technology. While other personality types might be intimidated by things that appear complex, C's are intrigued by them. C's prefer to know a lot versus others who want to know just enough to get by.

A **D**, for example, only wants to know information they perceive as useful right then. A **D** would say, "Don't show me how to build the clock, just show me how it works." **C**'s want to know it all and they store it away for future reference in case they need it someday. A **C** says, "Show me how to build the clock and don't leave out a single detail."

So if you are very knowledgeable about something, **C**'s are impressed. They love conversing with people who really know their stuff. And if you are flying by the seat of your pants, a **C** figures it out pretty quickly.

C's look before they leap

C's don't just jump into things like some personalities do. They look before they leap. They research a topic thoroughly and evaluate what they learned, and they check and double-check their findings before making a decision about whether to move forward. But once they do, that's the way they're going to do it no matter what.

I saw an example of this recently. I was in New York City and had dinner with a friend. I was riding the subway back to my hotel, when a couple got on carrying several suitcases. I could tell the wife was an **S** and the husband was a **C**. He remained with the suitcases, but his wife took a seat beside me. She kept glancing at the subway map in my hand. She asked others around her how they should get to their final destination. The husband kept talking to her in an aggravated tone.

Although he was speaking a different language, I knew exactly what he was saying. He had a binder in his hand that contained tons of maps. It was obvious he had spent a lot of time putting this binder together. He was saying to her, "I've got this figured out. I have already decided the correct way for us to go, so stop worrying."

And although several people on the subway tried to convince him there was a faster way, he wasn't going to hear it. He had already chosen the correct way in his mind, and nobody was going to sway him from that decision. I was thinking, "All of you are just wasting your breathe. This guy is not going to change his mind." And I was right.

So **C**'s can be stubborn, but generally, their research keeps them out of trouble because their decisions are usually right. Some other personality types could learn a thing or two about this **C** trait.

Brain benders

C's enjoy doing things that challenge their minds. They often do jigsaw puzzles or crosswords, or read the newspaper's "word of the day." They may look at the business section of the paper and review stock market standings. (An **I** type probably doesn't know such a thing exists, and if they do, they certainly aren't going to read it for laughs and giggles.)

Analytic people watchers

I'm sure you've guessed by now that **C**'s are very analytical in nature. They enjoy watching and analyzing other people. They take in their surroundings, evaluate them, and build a report in their mind that summarizes all that they have learned. Impressive, wouldn't you say?

Rules are there for a reason

Remember how the other three personality types stand on a street corner? To review, **D**'s are impatient foot tappers who may step into the intersection before the light changes. **I**'s window shop and chat with friends. **S**-types have friendly conversations with those around them and wish others a nice day.

C's are very different. They usually stare straight ahead and wait for the light to change. They wouldn't dare step into the intersection until the light turns green. That would be breaking the rules. "Rules were made to follow," thinks the **C**.

Planners

If you are disorganized or spontaneous, you may be annoying a **C**-type. They can't stand disorganization and they hate surprises. I've had **C**'s tell me they don't want a surprise gift, a surprise party, or any other type of surprise. They want to plan as much of their lives as possible. Big shock, right?

Everything must be just so

C's live by the motto, "A place for everything and everything in its place." Being organized is very important to them. Everything in their home is in a precise place and if someone moves something, even one inch, they will move it right back as soon as they notice (which won't take them long.)

> Some **C**'s put everything away at the end of the work day and take it all back out again the next day.

My friend's father is a high **C**, He's a retired research physician. One day, her father was showing some old Irish coins to her husband. He has them displayed in a glass case. Her husband picked up and looked at several of the coins and then put them back in the case. Her father spent the next several minutes rearranging them in the exact way (whatever that is, only he knows) they were in before his son-in-law messed things up. Her husband jokingly teased her father about it saying, "Can you say OCD?" (Obsessive Compulsive Disorder) Her father looked up with a blank stare. He had no idea what could possibly be funny—organization is serious business.

Since everything has a specific place, **C**'s also notice, right away, if you borrow something and don't return it. If they can, they lock the drawers of their desk at work and have areas at home that are off limits to others (particularly "formal" areas, which may be limited to adults only).

"Preparation" is their middle name

Have you ever met someone that was already prepared for a situation before it ever happened? **C**'s have a talent for being able to see down the road and figure out things they will need six months, even a year from now. This is the complete opposite of **D**-types who don't realize they need something until they need it.

C's also typically carry items that other personalities don't. C-type men often have a Swiss army knife with a corkscrew, file, bottle opener, and tiny scissors in their pockets. C-type women will likely keep "necessity kits," either in their drawer at work or in their purse. These kits contain items such as toothpicks, bandages, mints, a fingernail file, gum, floss, aspirin, a safety pin, and so on. So if you ever need something, go find a C. If they don't have it, they'll know where to get it.

Charts, graphs, and lists

Charts, graphs, and lists are a very important part of a C-types' lives and they don't understand why everyone doesn't use them. I's will make a list, but then leave it at home. S-types tend to spend a ton of time making lists of their lists, which causes D-types to think, "If you spent more time *doing* the stuff on the list instead of writing it down, your lists wouldn't be so darn long."

It's all about the results

C's are long-range goal setters and will stick to a dull routine for years, even if it's boring—as long as they know what the future result will be. I'm almost positive C-types were behind the planes that flew into the Twin Towers on September 11th. That catastrophe took years of detailed, meticulous planning. A D or an I would've been out of there as soon as it became boring.

Waste not want not

When it comes to buying that new luggage with wheels, a C may not jump at the latest and greatest. If their current luggage works just fine—just like the **S**-types—they believe it would be wasteful to get rid of a perfectly good suitcase just to get something new. They wait until their current luggage falls apart before they invest in something else.

Speaking of waste, my husband has a friend who is a **C/S** personality who was married to and then divorced from a woman from Thailand. A few years after their divorce, we were at his house visiting. I noticed a few beautiful pillows on his sofa that his ex wife had handmade while they were married. Typically, a **D** would never keep something like that after a relationship ends. I asked him why he still had them and he replied, "Well, they're nice pillows." In his mind, it would be wasteful to throw out something that still functioned.

Transfats, artificial flavors, and calories, oh my!

When **C**'s order food at a restaurant, they review, analyze, categorize, and break down the nutritional content of each dish on the entire menu before ordering. I was so glad to see several restaurants recently add the caloric intake for each item to their menus. This will save **C**'s a lot of time.

Germaphobes

Many **C**'s are germphobic. They almost always have some anti-bacterial soap within their reach. Occasionally, I'll see a **C** on a plane wearing a personal air purifier around their neck so they don't breathe in the stale, contaminated air on the plane. And they almost always use a paper towel to open a public bathroom door upon exiting. In a few restrooms, I've seen an invention that allows you to use your arm to open a door. This was definitely invented by a **C**.

When they travel, some C's take their own sheets with them instead of using the hotel sheets. (I hate to tell you this C's, but it's actually the comforter that never gets washed.) I've heard about C's ordering a cup of hot water at a restaurant to sterilize their utensils. Most cannot handle the thought of hot tubs. A high **C** friend calls hot tubs "germ-infested people stew." And I could write an entire book about C's and the nightmare called buffets. You C's out there are shuddering just thinking about them, aren't you?

Shake don't hug

Have you ever gone to hug someone and they stick their hand out instead? That person is most likely a **C**. They will not hug you unless you have a close relationship with them. If you try to hug them, they'll be stiff. It's like hugging a board. They'll also look very uncomfortable. That's because they are. They're thinking, "I don't know you that well and I certainly didn't plan to touch you today."

Fine arts and term papers

C's love poetry, art, literature, philosophy, and symphonies. And check this out I's, C's *enjoy* term papers and research projects. Can you imagine? I's bleed at the eyes at the mere suggestion that they do a term paper or research project (I'm with you on that one).

I can't hear myself think!

C's need to be in control of their work environment. They prefer to work in a place that is quiet and secluded. They can't function well in a chaotic, noisy environment. If you've ever heard someone say, "I can't hear myself think!" that's a **C**. They need quiet, uninterrupted thinking time (unlike **D**'s, who can work with bells, whistles, gunshots, and fireworks blasting in the background).

Skeptical

Have you ever met someone who didn't believe anything you said, no matter how much you tried to convince them? **C**'s must always verify what's being said. We'll talk more about this in the next chapter.

Clean cut, conservative dressers

When you look at a **C**-type, they usually appear one of two ways:

- Clean cut with every hair in place (they iron their blue jeans, by the way)
- Computer whizzy, Albert Einstein-y

It's a sure fire clue that someone's a **C** with the Einstein thing going on, if you see them wearing a pocket protector. For those of you who aren't familiar with this gadget, it's a plastic insert that goes inside the pocket on the front of a man's dress shirt. Its purpose is to keep pens from marking or staining the shirt. Every now and then I will still see a man—usually about 80 years old—wearing one. But whatever the age, or whoever's wearing one, they're probably a **C**.

C's also tend to dress in more conservative colors. If they wear a bright color, it's for one of two reasons. One, they got it on sale or two, they're married to an **I** who bought it for them.

One time, my husband saw a man at church who was wearing a bright pink shirt. After the service, my husband walked up to him and said, "You must be an **I**." First of all, the man had no idea what my husband was talking about. To make it worse, the man was a **C** and was now wondering what my husband just called him. Turns out, he was married to an **I** who bought his clothes for him, and although he didn't care for the color, he thought it would be a waste not to wear the shirt.

Extreme organization

A **C**'s closet is usually extremely organized. They'll have all their dress shirts together and all their casual shirts together. Each clothing item is turned the same direction. They may have clothes arranged "darks to lights" in the fall and "lights to darks" in the spring. I have met some **C**'s that have areas assigned for their shoes; spring shoes are not allowed to touch fall shoes.

There is not a cheap wire hanger anywhere in the closet, unless it has dry cleaning hanging on it. They may even have different colored coat hangers for every member of the family (pink for Mom, brown for Dad , white for Krissy, blue for Justin). If you are a **C** and you don't do that, then right about now you may be thinking, "That is a great idea. Thanks!" You are welcome.

The **C**-type's pantry is usually tidy as well. They put their cans of soups together, their cans of fruits together, their cans of vegetables together, and so on. Every label is turned to the front. Sometimes they write the date on their cans and food packages so they can rotate them so that nothing expires.

I have also seen **C**'s organize their pantry by weight. They put the heaviest items on the bottom. That way if the shelf falls, it won't have so far to go. And they often alphabetize their spices from A to Z. Seriously.

Their garages are immaculate. They have plastic storage bins labeled "Sprinkler Parts," "Christmas Decorations," "Light Bulbs," "Paint Supplies," and on and on.

> If you want to mess with the **C**, take a can of beans and stick it in with the cans of fruit.

And the labels aren't just messily drawn on with a marker. They're produced on a computer using a readable font and printed out on fresh white labels that are adhered on the side of each box, in the exact center.

Slow and steady wins the race

C's spend a lot of time on a job making sure whatever it is, is done just right. Quality over quantity every time. Unlike the fast-moving **D**'s and **I**'s, **C**'s (who are like **S**-types in this respect) take as much time as they need to do the job to the best of their abilities. They strive for perfection. They prefer to be systematic and do things in a particular order. They typically focus on one project at a time.

A friend of mine has a husband who is a high **C**. Recently, I asked her how her weekend was. She rolled her eyes and told me that, on Saturday, they were supposed to go boating, but her husband spent almost an entire day installing a new sink in the bathroom to replace the old, cracked one. It took him three hours to plan everything out, an hour to go to the hardware store and buy the parts he needed, and three hours to install it. He did, she admitted, a fantastic job. It was perfect. Slow and steady wins the race, right Mr. Turtle?

Pack rats

C's save items they think they can use in the future—particularly electronic items. They may have old computer towers, CB radios, turntables, or any other thing they think may come in handy one day. Some call C's pack rats.

This is the opposite thinking from a **D**, who discards things they haven't used in a very short period. In fact, my favorite day of the week is garbage day because I get to watch lots of stuff go away that is no longer needed.

Thrifty not cheap

C's love to pinch pennies. Some might call them cheap, but they prefer "thrifty" or, better yet, "cost conscious." And they find a use for almost everything.

Several years ago, I worked at an office in Florida that was hit by a hurricane. The roof was torn off and many things were destroyed. After the storm, we began sorting through items to throw out. I was excited that all the garbage would be going away. When I started to throw away a three-ring binder that was missing the entire back cover, a **C**-type person in the office said, "Wait, I can use that for something." I thought, "Oh boy, I'd hate to see all the 'treasures' (junk) he'll be taking home to his poor wife."

If you ever see someone at the end of your driveway digging through your trash, or hauling away that desk with two legs that you put out there, rest assured, it's probably a **C**.

C's also love to clip coupons and get rebates. **I**-types like to as well, but then they leave them all at home and wind up with piles of expired coupons. **D** types? Not so much on the coupons. Time spent clipping is better spent doing something else—anything else.

Friends versus acquaintances

You may remember that I told you that after an **I**-type has talked to someone for five minutes, they're introducing them as their new friend. Not the **C**. The **C**-type is very careful about who they call a friend. They know many people they would call an "acquaintance," but they reserve the term friend for only those who are very close to them.

Serious faces

If you watch the facial expressions of a **C**-type, you might not see a whole lot, which in itself is actually helpful in identifying them. **C**'s tend to have few facial expressions. When they do, it's often a furrowed brow, because they're thinking about something or weighing options. There is nothing animated or smiley about the **C**-type. They wear their "serious face" proudly.

Question everything

C's also tend to ask a lot of questions. But guess what? You'll never answer all of their questions. Once you have answered one set of questions, they review and analyze the information you gave them, and return the next day with a whole new set. Funny, huh? "Not really," some of you are thinking.

Compassionate and sensitive

C-types are compassionate people and very sensitive to the needs of others. **D**'s, including myself, could learn to display a little more of this trait perhaps.

More about C's

C's also:

- Are fact-oriented
- Are very detail-oriented
- Marvel at the wonders of nature
- Tend to seek the perfect mate (does that exist?)

As you can tell, there are many great things about **C**'s. The world is a much more organized place with them in it.

In the next chapter, I'll cover a few pitfalls for the **C**-type. If you are a **C**, read the next chapter objectively. Don't worry, I'm not being critical. I only want to help.

🔔 CHAPTER 10 🔔

The Challenging Side of C

A re you starting to think of a few **C**'s that you know? As we learned in the last chapter, there are many great things about being a **C**.

Unfortunately, some people get annoyed by the **C**'s **C**-ness. They think **C**'s are inflexible, unemotional, critical, unfriendly, judgmental, uncaring, anal retentive, perfectionist whiners. That's a bit harsh.

Okay **C**'s, take a deep breath. It's time to look at *your* under control and out of control list. Again, this is not meant to be critical. I know that you are going to choose the correct word for you because you are great at being right.

Under Control	Out of Control
Orderly	Compulsive
Logical	Critical
Intense	Unsociable
Curious	Prying
Teachable	Easily offended
Cautious	Fearful
Correct	Inflexible
Questioning	Doubtful
Conscientious	Worrisome
Precise	Picky

I'm not going to do it if I can't do it right

C's tend to be perfectionists by nature. This is not necessarily a bad thing but, taken to extremes, it can be. **C**'s have very high expectations of others, and of themselves. When they don't live up to their own perfectionist standards, they get upset. When **C**'s think they can't do something perfectly, they don't want to do it at all. This trait keeps **C**'s, sometimes, from wanting to try new things. **C**'s say things like, "I'm not good at that," or "I've never done that before. Get someone else to do it."

Don't be afraid to try new things—even if you can't do them perfectly. Remember, everything you do now was new to you at one point.

And because **C**'s are perfectionists, they tend to put unrealistic demands on others. **C**'s, try to relax. No one is perfect. Be accepting of others and have realistic standards.

What do you mean by that?

Have you ever met someone who is skeptical about *everything*? Then you've probably met a C-type. C's don't take anything at face value. They're always digging for the truth. To them, whatever someone says cannot possibly be what they really mean. You may catch them asking, "What did you mean by that?"

For example, if I say to a C, "I really like your shirt," they immediately think, "What did she mean by that? Does she want something? Did she not like my shirt yesterday? What, exactly, does she mean?"

To any other personality type it would mean, "She likes my shirt." But, again, C's tend to think four levels deep about everything.

What's the score?

Some C types (not all) "keep score" when they lend you something. C's know who owes who half a stick of butter, a cup of milk, and spoonful of sugar. There's most likely a log with it documented somewhere.

And, they expect you to return more than you borrowed. For example, if they lend you their boat and there's half a tank of gas in it, C's would expect the tank to be full when you return it. Why? Because, to them, it's all about the big picture.

Let's take a look at the situation from a C's perspective. They think, "You're going to put hours on my engine, so I am going to have to service the boat sooner. And you certainly aren't going to clean the boat the way I expect it to be kept, so I'll need to clean it."

The lesson? If you are borrowing something from a C, always return more than you borrow so that they're more likely to lend you things in the future.

If you are a C, try not to keep score.

Beware of black clouds

You'll know when **C**'s are in a bad mood. You can almost see a black cloud hovering over them. And **C**-type bad moods tend to last for a long period of time.

It's okay to have a bad day, but understand it may not be a good day to be around others. Try to keep yourself and your big black cloud from raining on everyone else's parade.

Negative + negative = negative

If **C**-types hear their name in a conversation they often think, "Is someone talking bad about me?" **C**'s do this because they tend to focus on the negative instead of the positive. Although this can come in handy, in certain respects, it doesn't always.

If you are a **C**, don't make assumptions. Get the facts before you jump to conclusions. Try not to always see the negative in everything. Look for the positives. Don't take things personally. Stop thinking everyone is out to get you. Try not to be so easily hurt.

Preparation or procrastination?

Preparation. That is what the **C**-type calls it. Unfortunately, everyone elsc calls it "procrastination." **C**'s tend to not begin a project until they have everything they need from beginning to end to complete it. It usually takes longer to *plan* the project than it would've taken to just *do* the project.

Try to get started on projects right away and gather things that you need as you go.

Participate or be left out

Because **C**'s tend to be more reserved in nature, when someone asks them to participate in something, or join them for an event, they often say no. After this happens several times, people may stop asking them to go. This causes the **C** to feel left out.

Try to participate in things, even if you may not feel like it. Trust me, you'll have a good time.

What's wrong with me?

C's do not like to play games and goof off. They don't like to smile in the morning and they don't think life is very funny. Because of this, **C**'s sometimes ask, "What's wrong with me?" They wonder why they

> **C**'s get annoyed, at times, by the light-hearted attitudes of **I** types.

can't act goofy like the **I**'s. Nothing is wrong with you. You are just wired differently.

Here's something to think about. The most prescribed drugs in the United States right now are anti-depressants—which is astounding considering all of the types of drugs that exist. **C**-types must be careful about not turning to medication because they can't act like **I**'s. I'm not saying, by the way, that all **C**'s are medicated. I'm just saying, be careful with your perception of you and don't take drastic steps to try to be like someone else.

More about C's

C's also:

- Are sometimes paralyzed by their own over analysis
- Can be critical of others
- Often give too much information

C affirmations

Following are some great affirmations for **C**'s to write three times each as you start your day:

- I am flexible and forgiving.
- I am great at considering the opinion of others.
- I work quickly and efficiently.
- I am productive no matter what my surroundings are.
- I am a multitasker.
- I am fun and full of energy!

C's, you are wonderful people. Your deeper look at things saves you tons of money and keeps you from jumping into "get rich quick" schemes. You bring so much value and knowledge to the world. Just try to be a little more flexible, and you'll continue to be a great, great person.

CHAPTER 11

Getting Along with the Dominant D

People often ask me, "What is the best gift I can give to a **D**?" Honestly? Money. Really. **D**'s prefer to buy their own gifts. Give them money so they can get what they really want. They will love you for it.

Don't ask them the same question twice

D's believe that you should only have to say something once and that should be enough. They have a low tolerance for repetition. They think things such as, "When we got married, I told you I loved you. If anything changes, I'll be sure to let you know."

This is the only personality style that is not repetitive; all others are but for different reasons. (I'll cover them in their respective chapters.)

Don't waste their time

Because **D**'s are all about results, make sure you don't waste their time. They want you to get to the bottom line and get there quickly. They want you to be brief, be brilliant, and be gone. They are not interested in jokes and small talk—it's all about results and action.

Ask what they think, not how they feel

It's not a good idea to come on too strong with a **D**. This can be a challenge if you are a **D** living or working with another **D**.

When you are dealing with a **D**-type, they may challenge you. Do not take this personally or get offended. **D**'s make decisions based on logic, not emotion. Until it makes sense in their head, they will not move forward. If they are challenging you, it usually means there is interest, so have thick skin and hang in there.

D's are logical in nature. They are thinkers. So, ask them what they "think" about something, not how they "feel." In fact, if you were to ask them how they feel about something, their response would probably be something like, "Well, I *think*....."

Stick to the bottom line

Since **D**'s are very bottom line-oriented, they do not want information that they perceive as useless. They become bored or aggravated quickly, especially if they feel their time is being wasted. Get to the point—even if you are an **S** or a **C** and don't understand how they can possibly proceed without knowing all of the information that you think is important.

And **D**'s are not accustomed to two-way communication. They tell you what they think and, to them, that's the end of the conversation.

Deliver bad news asap

If you have bad news to deliver to a **D**-type, do it as fast as possible. The worst thing that can happen is for the **D** to find out that you have known something for two weeks and you are just now telling them. And, don't worry too much about breaking the news—they are probably going to fix it any way.

Know your stuff

Be organized and knowledgeable when working with **D**'s. They don't tolerate inefficiency and cannot stand to work with someone who appears ignorant. Know and show your stuff.

Use D words

D's like status and prestige, so present information with this in mind. Use words that **D**-types are attracted to such as grand, powerful, greatest, best, biggest, fast, quick, challenging, thrilling, bold, dramatic, increased productivity. Get the picture?

So, if you are a real estate agent and you are representing a house for sale where a famous movie star lives two doors away, definitely mention that to a **D**. Or, if you are a car salesperson and a **D** is looking at a sports car, use the same principle. Again, it's all about status and prestige.

Give them choices

When dealing with **D**'s, it's best to give them choices, but let *them* make the decision. The three things that this personality wants are: choices, challenge, and control.

Compete but don't challenge

Do you want a **D** to be excited about doing something? Make it competitive. They love a challenge. The harder, the better. This is the environment they thrive in.

But although **D**'s like challenges, and love to challenge others, they don't want to *be* challenged, so it's a good idea to approach them in a very non-threatening way. Try to figure out a way to make them think that your great idea was *their* great idea. They wouldn't dare say no to their own idea.

Take issue with the facts, not the person

If you have a disagreement with a **D**, take issue with the facts, not the person. Avoid bringing extra things into the discussion that really have nothing to do with the issue.

Bullet points are best

When you are writing to a **D**-type, do not send lots of text or use small print. Communicate with bullet points, if possible. They view this as very efficient and, by being efficient, you will win their hearts (yes, believe it or not, **D**'s do have hearts).

Move quickly

Above all, move quickly when dealing with a **D**. Remember, they believe time is money. The worst thing you can do is have them think you are wasting their time.

CHAPTER 12

Getting Along with the Inspiring I

The best gift for an **I**, in case you're wondering, is…anything. They absolutely love getting gifts so much they don't really care what it is. They're just thrilled that you gave them something.

Be patient

I's repeat things a lot. They don't mean to; they honestly forget what they just said. They'll say the same things over and over as if they have never said them before. This can be very annoying to a **D** personality (who only wants to hear things once).

Be bottom line

I's are bottom line-oriented when *receiving* information. They do not want you to tell them a bunch of information that they perceive as boring and useless. Of course, when an **I** is *giving* information, they can talk for hours.

Use I words

I's make decisions based on emotion, so they are easily influenced. If you have their attention long enough, you can pretty much talk them into anything. Like **D**'s, they also are interested in status and prestige. Here are some words that **I**'s are attracted to: fabulous, fantastic, endless opportunities, fun, exciting, tempting, fun-filled, hilarious, romantic.

Relax your writing

Do you have someone in your life that forwards you about 50 joke e-mails a day? That person is, most likely, an **I**-type. **I**'s love to laugh and to make others laugh. Unfortunately, they lack the SA (situational awareness) that not everyone has time to read that many e-mails—except another **I**.

When you are writing to an **I**, be very relaxed in your writing style. They love when you mention that someone said to tell them, "Hi," or asked about them. Shower them with compliments and make them feel like they are the star of the show. Go out of your way to be friendly with **I**-types and they will tell all of their **I** friends how wonderful you are.

Ask questions

Because **I**'s love to talk, ask them questions. Ask them about themselves or their interests. If you ask them one question, they usually will talk for a long time, so it's really not that hard.

Be flexible

Flexibility is key when you are dealing with an **I**. Being flexible is harder to do for some personalities than others. Try to keep plans flexible, or have no plans at all. They love to do things on the spur of the moment and don't want everything planned out in advance. If they feel like getting ice cream, they want to do it right then. Allow time for socializing and just going with the flow.

Paint a picture

If you want to motivate an **I** to do something, just paint a picture that shows how doing it will make them look good. For example, if you're a realtor, say things like, "Your friends are going to be so jealous when they pull into the driveway of this home." This will get their visual wheels turning right away.

Reward instantly

If you are going to give an **I** something in exchange for doing something good, you must give them instant rewards. For example, if you say to an **I** child, "If you are good at school all week, on Friday I'll give you 20 dollars," they will not even try. To them, five days is an eternity. It's an unreachable goal. Instead, give them a smaller reward every day. If you ask them to complete a task at home, give them a reward immediately after, instead of offering an allowance or rewarding at the end of the week.

Get excited

I's are great at verbalizing ideas. They love to talk about how fun things would be to do. If you want to make them happy, get excited with them. But understand that, although I's might have every intention of doing what they are talking about, something else comes along and they'll focus their attention on that for a while. Again, they saw something shiny.

Give them the stage

I's want to be part of friendly relationships. They thrive on opportunities to influence or inspire others because it makes them feel important. Give them the stage and they will win over everyone in the room. This is where they shine, so don't be afraid to put them in the spotlight.

Recognize them

Similarly, I's love public recognition. Stroke their ego and they will bend over backwards to help you. Tell them how great they are and they will feel on top of the world. (Of course, if you do this too much, their head will become so big they may have trouble fitting through the door.)

Ask them how they feel

I's are feelers, so don't bother asking them what they think about something, just go straight to how they feel. This will help them process their emotions more quickly. When you ask an I to think, you're asking them to go somewhere that is not natural to them, since they make their decisions on how they feel.

Don't talk each other to death

If you are an **I** and you have an **I** customer, try not to talk each other to death. I've met some **I**'s who have lots of "customers," but never sell anything. They may have a great time, but they've forgotten to accomplish the task. Remember to keep on track when dealing with another **I**. One of you has to get it done.

Make a fuss and make it fun

Above all, make it fun. **I**'s love big productions, especially over them. They adore it when you make a fuss. If it's their birthday, they'd love if you planned a big surprise party, or put their name on a marquee in front of your building, or filled their office with balloons, or rented a limo to take them to dinner. All of these will score major points with an **I**.

CHAPTER 13

Getting Along with the Supportive S

In terms of the best gift for an **S**, make it something sentimental. This is the personality that actually appreciates those handmade items. As a high **S**, my husband loves things that are sentimental. This past Valentine's Day, I wrote him a poem and put it in a card I made. You would have thought I gave him a million dollars. He was so happy. He crowed about how talented I was telling me that not everyone can write a poem. As a **D** I'm thinking, "What's the big deal? It only took me five minutes." But I definitely got a good return on that investment of time.

In fact, the best gift I give him at Christmas each year costs me less than 20 dollars. I make him one of those calendars that you can put pictures on. I include pictures of things we did during that month. I even put everyone's picture on the date of their birthdays. He has every calendar I have ever given him lined up along the wall in our home office. Each month, he looks forward to going into the office and turning all the calendars to the next month. Every once in a while, he'll call me into the office and say something like, "Look at this, sweetheart. Here's where we were two years ago, and here's where we were three years ago…" As a **D**, I'm thinking, "Yes, honey, I know. I made the calendar."

S words

Just like all other personality types, **S**-types have words that they respond best to. Their words do not involve status and prestige, however. This personality type is motivated by safety and security. Here are some words that attract them: relaxing, guaranteed, user-friendly, easy-to-use, time-saving, effortless, soothing.

And, because **S**-types love to feel like they are a part of something, use the word "we" often when you are talking to them. They respond better to feeling included.

Go with the known, not the new

The tried, the true, the stable, the proven. Those are things that make an **S** feel comfortable. Because they are more comfortable with the known and expected, don't stress the "new" of things. Also, if there's a problem that you need to talk to an **S** about, it's best if you also go in with the solution.

Ask about family

If you really want to score major points with **S**-types, ask about their family. They will be so happy that you took the time to care about them. Always start your conversations with a personal comment.

Discuss personal feelings

Since disagreements are something that an **S** tries to avoid, if you happen to have conflict with them, discuss your personal feelings and how their decisions are going to affect their own personal circumstances. Remember, everything is personal to an **S**.

Ask them how they feel

Like **I**'s, **S**-types are also feelers. So ask them how they feel about something instead of asking what they think about it. They make decisions based on emotion, not logic, so jump straight to the emotion.

Listen

Really listen when **S**-types are talking, and show support for their decisions (remember how hard it was for them to make the decision in the first place). When you are talking to them, present information softly, but don't be vague. They like a lot of details but need them to be easy to understand.

Relax your writing

As with an **I**, when you are writing or e-mailing an **S**, be more relaxed and casual in your writing style. They will often e-mail you a reminder of your appointment or plans that you have with them, so surprise them by e-mailing them first. They will think, "That's just what I was going to do. They are so like me."

Touch them

This personality usually loves physical touch, so give them a hug or a shoulder rub. They will appreciate that you took the time to show them attention like this. Major points will be scored.

Determine their true wants and desires

Another challenge, when it comes to an **S**, is trying to figure out their true wants and desires. What makes this even harder is that *they* don't even know. They just know something is not right.

The most effective way to figure out their true wants and desires is by repeating back to them whatever they say in the form of a question. For example, let's say you are a male **D**-type married to an **S**. When you come home from work, your wife says, "I have a headache." The natural **D** response is, "Take some aspirin." More than likely, if this is your response, your **S** wife will say something like, "You just don't understand me!" Instead, try this:

She:	I have a headache.
You:	Oh, sweetheart, you have a headache?
She:	I have been working in this house all day.
You:	Oh, honey, you've been working all day?
She:	Yes, and I am so exhausted!
You:	I'm sorry, baby, you're exhausted?
She:	Yes, and I'm just too tired to cook dinner.
You:	Oh, sweetheart, you don't want to cook?
She:	No, let's go out.

Do you see that it wasn't about the headache? It was about how tired she was and how she didn't feel like she could do another thing that day. She didn't know this herself, at the time, but you helped her work through it by asking questions.

After I told this story in one of my seminars, a man in the **D** section raised his hand. When I called on him he asked, "So if my wife says she has a headache, I should ask her if she wants a salad?" Hmm, I don't think he got the point. Hopefully *you* do.

D-types, you naturally think, "That is such a monumental waste of time. Why can't she just tell me what she wants so I can fix it?" You need to learn to view it as an *investment* of time because, the reality is, you will spend more time fighting about the fact that you don't understand your spouse if you don't do this. Instead, you will actually save time *and* have a happy spouse.

Keep it simple

S-types are very A to Z and like to process information before giving an answer. They want to consider all of the data they receive so they can give their best response. The result? A slow, but accurate answer. This is difficult for **D**'s who want quick responses from everyone.

S-types also want information to be very easy to understand, so keep it simple. Give them time to digest the information, and ask questions.

Don't be so down to business

Remember, everything is personal to an **S**. Because of this, you cannot call an **S** on the phone and have a conversation using *your* personality style. For example, let's say you're a **D** and you need a phone number. You call your **S** spouse to get the information. You say, "Yeah, I just need the phone number I wrote on the notepad on my desk." Then, after you receive it, you say, "Thanks. Bye." That's a typical **D** conversation.

If you do this to an **S**, they will be devastated. They will think something like, "Oh my goodness, they didn't even want to talk to me. I must have upset them. Something is wrong. I have to fix this right away. I don't know what happened."

To make an **S** happy, you must have an **S** conversation. Here's the same conversation in **S** language:

> **D:** Hi, sweetheart! I'd really love to talk to you right now, but I am so under the gun. Could you just give me (whatever you need) real quick? I promise we'll talk again later.
>
> **S:** Sure, it's (whatever it is).
>
> **D:** Thank you so much! You're a life saver. I love you! Talk to you soon. Goodbye!

After you hang up, the **S** thinks, "Aw, he loves me. I helped him and we are going to talk again later. I can't wait. Life is so great."

Are you beginning to see how being able to speak different personality languages is beneficial?

CHAPTER 14

Getting Along with the Cautious C

Since we started off by talking about the best gift to give each of the other personalities in the previous three chapters, we should do that for the **C** as well. Because if we change the order of things, they'll get flustered. (Just teasing.) The absolute best gift you can give a **C** is…a label maker. Really. They *love* them.

When my husband and I were first married, it was obvious that he did not understand my **D/I** personality because he got *me* a label maker. When I opened the gift, as a **D**, I thought, "A label maker? Money would have been so much better." The label maker sat its package for years.

One day, my high **I** daughter and I were kidding around. She said, "While Dad's out of town, let's get out the label maker and start labeling everything: the forks, the drawers, the appliances. Everything. We can even label the label maker. Wouldn't that be a riot?" We laughed ourselves silly.

C words

As with the other personality types, certain words or phrases appeal to **C**-types. Examples include: perfect, impeccable, meticulous, money-saving, tailored to fit your needs, details included, everything you need to know, organized, systematic, intellectual, sensitive, automatic, perfectly-engineered.

No surprises

One thing that **C**'s do not like are surprises. They prefer to plan everything in their lives. If you don't understand this, there could be big trouble in Dodge. For example, you are a high **I**, and you are in a relationship with a **C**-type. Your **C**'s birthday is coming up soon so you decide you are going to plan a surprise party. You are going to call all of your friends to meet at a restaurant and, when your **C** walks in, you'll all yell, "Surprise!" You think, "This is going to be great!" Actually, no, it won't. In fact, it will be the opposite of great.

One time, I was talking about this in a seminar and a man in the **I** section of the room exclaimed, "Oh no, the party is tonight!" We all laughed. He was serious. We all felt very sorry for him.

Don't take third-party validation personally

C's have a need for third-party validation. As I mentioned earlier, in their minds, whatever you say is not to be believed. Recently, I taught a seminar in upstate New York. As soon as I started talking about this, an **I**'s hand shot up. She said, "That's my husband! He thinks I never tell him the truth and he wants to research everything I say, or ask someone else if what I say is true. It's so frustrating." I'll tell you what I told her. Do not take it personally. It's not about you, it's just how **C**-types are wired. If you want to get along with a **C**, understand their need for validation and allow them the liberty to do so.

Don't kid around

Because this personality is suspicious by nature, you cannot kid around with them the way you can the other personality types. Keep joking to a minimum unless they joke about things first.

Don't point and laugh

C's also don't like attention drawn to them. So, if they happen to walk out of the bathroom with toilet paper stuck to their shoe, don't point and laugh hysterically. Instead, pretend that it's not there and do a quick "step and release."

Be calm, rational, systematic, and prepared

Try not to get over excited with **C**-types. They prefer calm and rational discussions. If you get excited or wound up around them, they often get flustered.

Additionally, be systematic and well prepared when working with **C**'s. They value knowledge and want to see yours. Have the facts and figures they need to make a decision ready. Use charts, graphs, numbers, and lists whenever possible.

Be sure to support their methodical approach. When I was selling real estate, I had a **C**-type that drew a smiley face for everything he liked about each house and a sad face for everything he didn't like about each one. At the end of the day, the house with the most smiley faces is the one he bought.

Ask what they think, not feel

C's make decisions based on logic, so ask what they think about something instead of how they feel. Discuss logical solutions. They are not persuaded with emotion.

It's okay to be quiet

If you're around a **C**-type it's fine if you are not talking all of the time (that's right **I**'s, you can be quiet and it's okay). They are good with quiet. In fact, they actually enjoy it.

Be on time

C-types, try to keep a reasonable schedule and they expect others to do the same. They don't like change, so don't move deadlines or meeting times if at all possible. They've already planned everything out so that things will be accomplished perfectly by the time you originally told them.

Include everything

When you are sending an e-mail or providing information to a **C**-type, I'm pretty sure it's not possible to make it too long. They love loads of information. Give them all the details, even if you don't think they are important. If they are a potential client, tell them how long you have been in business, how your company compares to others, what your qualifications are, and so on. Let *them* decide what they need and what they don't (they'll probably think they need it all).

Slow and measured

C's don't like to make quick decisions, and don't move at a fast pace, so when working with them, present information slowly. Give them a chance to digest facts. Allow time for questions.

Do what you say you'll do

C's don't care what you *say* you are going to do, they care about what you actually *do*. Demonstrate through actions rather than words.

CHAPTER 15

Explaining the Personality Blends

I'm now going to discuss the various personality blends. See if you can figure out where you fit. Two examples of blends are **natural blends and complimentary blends**, as described in following table.

Personality Blends and Strengths

Blend Type	Personality Type	Strengths
Natural	D/I or I/D	Live in extremes; emotions change quickly
	S/C or C/S	Emotions change slowly
Complimentary	D/C or C/D	Great business leaders due to their drive to achieve and their organizational skills
	I/S or S/I	Best in dealing with people; very easy to get along with

Opposite Blends

Some people may tell you that they're an **I/C** or an **S/D**. These are called **opposite blends**. People are not born as opposite blends; they develop into them over time. For example, let's say you are an **I/C** blend. Either you have:

- Learned to goof off and have fun, or
- Learned to be organized

You have not been one of these two your entire life. Each time I explain this to someone, they're able to tell me instantly which one is learned.

I just love the **I/C** blend (think Howie Mandel). I had an **I/C** in a class one time who did something I'll never forget. In this particular class, I gave each student a container of PlayDoh˚. As an **I**, this person was having a great time playing with it, but at the same time, his **C** side was explaining to others that the PlayDoh is sodium-based, which is what causes it to dry out.

Level personalities

As I mentioned at the beginning of the book, sometimes people test level, which means that they are fairly even in all four types. Again, they were not born this way. They just have incorporated traits from other personalities so much, that those traits have become natural to them.

What does this mean? This person can be anywhere and fit in comfortably *for a short period*. They could be in a business meeting, at a party, consoling a friend, or doing finances and none of these would make them uncomfortable, as long as it's brief.

Level individuals are harder to read from a profiler's perspective because they don't stand out as much as someone who is dominant in one or two of the personalities.

Everyone has some of all four

We each have traits of all four personalities to some degree. Everyone has the ability to operate under all four—you just might not choose to do so very often. For example, if you were to take out a pen and write your name, that would be very comfortable. But if you put the pen in your opposite hand and write your name, you are no longer comfortable (unless you are ambidextrous).

What if I asked you to remove your shoes but put them back on beginning with the foot you normally do last? Most people would be very uncomfortable doing this. This is similar to operating within your lowest two personality types.

We tend to stay within our dominant personalities.

Work versus home

I'm asked a lot, "Why am I one way at home and another at work?" The answer is simple. We tend to stay within our most dominant personality type until one of two things happen:

- Your most dominant trait is satisfied
- Your most dominant trait is not going to work for you in
  a situation

For example, I am a high **D/I** blend (meaning that my **D** comes first). I cannot jump to my **I** until my **D** is satisfied; that is, I must first complete all of my tasks and anything else my **D** side wants done. After that, I can have fun, just like any other **I**.

The other scenario is if I'm in a situation and my **D** is not going to cut it, I jump to my **I**. Let's say that I'm a realtor at a listing appointment. If

I can see that I'm probably not going to get the listing, I may jump to my **I** and start telling jokes to liven up the room a bit. The amazing thing is, this happens without us ever knowing it most of the time.

I, of course, can do this consciously because it's a by-product of my profession. If I'm talking to a **C**-type, I know that neither my **D** nor **I** will work, so I'll need to give a lot of details and allow time for questions.

Remember, the easiest way to find out your personality blend is by going to **www.personalityprofiles.org**, clicking on "Order Materials," and then clicking on "Assessments" to take an online assessment. It will give you valuable insights into your personality type. While there, click on "Personality Pointer" to sign up for my free bi-weekly newsletter, which contains tips and tricks on using the profiling tool. It also, from time to time, offers special prices on assessments.

⚔ CHAPTER 16 ⚔

Does My Personality Ever Change?

The answer is yes. You are born a particular personality and, no, it has nothing to do with your birth order. Often, this misconception exists because parents tend to expect a lot from their first-born children and, therefore, raise them as if they are **D**'s. Eventually this could make a child exhibit many **D** traits. Usually by the time parents get to a third child, they are too worn out to raise them the same way they did their first one, so those children tend to get away with a lot more. This is why it's so important for parents to understand the personalities of their children. Two great books discuss this in detail.

- *Different Children, Different Needs*, by Charles Boyd
- *Personality Insights For Moms*, by Susan Crook

You can order both books on my Web site. Go to **www.personality profiles.org** and click on "Order Materials."

Factors that shape and mold your personality

Even though you are born a particular personality, you may not die the same personality. Three factors shape and mold your personality over your lifetime. They are:

- Experiences
- Environment
- Culture

Any situation you can name will fit into one of these three categories. They could be good or bad, but they will shape you just the same.

Experiences

Perhaps you were born an **S**, but your parents died very young and you had to raise your siblings. Out of necessity, you might become more **D**. I know people who experienced a traumatic event in their lives and their personalities changed instantly, and they never went back to the way they originally were.

Environment

The **D** personalities I teach in New York City are far more aggressive than the **D** personalities I teach in Key West. Out of necessity, we adapt to our environment.

Culture

D American women are far more aggressive than **D** women of some other cultures. It's not acceptable for a woman to be aggressive in every culture, so even though she may be born a **D**, her **D**-ness must be subdued out of necessity.

Assess yourself for changes

I suggest that you do an assessment once a year to see if there is anything going on that is affecting your personality. Often, things are going on that we haven't owned up to yet.

I will never forget a seminar I did in Canada. A gentleman in the class, who is normally a high **I/D** blend, took an assessment that revealed he hadn't been having much fun lately. When I questioned him about it, he didn't acknowledge what I was saying. Later that evening, I attended a dinner where he was present along with his wife. She asked me what his personality blend was and when I told her he was an **I/D**. She said, "That's what I thought he would be, but he just hasn't been as much fun lately." Even though others were able to notice this in him, he had not yet come to grips with it himself.

To take an assessment, go to my Web site at **www.personalityprofiles. org**, click on "Order Materials," and then on the "Assessments" button. Assessments are available for kids, teens, and adults. With all of the assessments, you will answer 24 questions and it will take you about 15 to 20 minutes to complete. You'll receive a 48-page report for kids and adults and a 58-page report for teens (you need more help with the teenagers, I guess).

CHAPTER 17

This Could Be You!

his chapter is all about people, just like you, who started out not understanding anything about our different personality types and, after attending one of my seminars, or being exposed to some of my materials, they quickly discovered how life-changing this information can be. See if you can find yourself within this chapter; there's probably someone that you can relate to.

Janet

Janet recognized the importance of teachers understanding this information to benefit the kids in their class. If you happen to be a teacher, there are tons of great resources available on my Web site. Just click on the "Order Materials" button to see all of the great items available.

Here's what Janet had to say:

Angel's insight into my personality, as well as helping me determine other people's personalities, has helped me tremendously. In my business, I know how to serve a customer better. Personally, life with my children, friends, and a significant other has improved. It's much easier to keep a relationship on an even plane if you understand that it's sometimes just their personality, and not personal. Everyone should be required to take this type of training, especially teachers, because they are working with little personalities that need structure and training, and need to realize that not all children can be treated the same.

Janet DiChiara

Medina, TN

Leigh

Leigh-attended a seminar I taught in Toronto, Canada for business owners. Here's what she had to say:

My life has changed in many ways since I met Angel Tucker. My husband and I opened a franchise in April, 2006. In Toronto, I attended Angel's fascinating seminar about understanding different personalities. My life has never been the same. I understand and accept myself for the first time.

I always knew I loved being alone and being highly productive all day. I like taking on a big task such as reorganizing my entire kitchen, or repainting a room. At work, I love to plan projects. The more I accomplish in a day, the better. When I have checklists, I can do anything better. I don't like to delegate because nobody can do anything as well as I can. I don't know how to relax or enjoy leisure time. To just sit and "be" is a waste of time. My entire day is planned and scheduled. I am abrupt and direct when I speak to people.

At other times, I thrive on interacting and communicating with people. My laugh fills the room. I tell entertaining stories and wave my hands in descriptive gestures. My excitement and optimism know no bounds. I want to go everywhere with everyone and do everything. I get so excited about socializing, my objectivity goes out the window. I am an eternal optimist. Let's laugh and have fun!

I never thought it was okay to have these extreme personality traits. It felt like I was too far to one side and too far on the other side. I thought there must be something wrong with me because I was so out of balance.

Angel taught me about personality profiles. I learned that I have equal **D** *and* **I** *personality styles and that this is okay; it's just how I'm wired. I'm not flawed or mildly insane. I have learned more and more about myself over the years. I know that when I have satisfied my* **D**, *I can be the most full on* **I**. *What would have happened if I had not ever learned my personality profile? I might have always thought there was something wrong with me.*

Knowing my personality profile has changed my relationship with my husband. Nothing bothers him, ever. He has measured responses. He never hits the panic button. His range of emotions is limited. At times, this can make me feel, "Why doesn't he care about anything? Where's his sense of urgency? How can he be so calm?"

I now understand that his **S** *personality traits allow him to tolerate my intense passions. I need this trait in my husband to survive in a marriage. If he reacted in high gear, the way I do, we would be too volatile to have any peace. In a nutshell, he puts up with me. What a blessing that I have him! He's a wonderful husband, and I now appreciate our differences.*

Since I do the interviewing for our office, understanding personality profiles has been invaluable. I can sum up an agent very quickly. It's fascinating to use for interviewing. The clothing a person wears, their neatness (or lack of), jewelry style, body language, choice of words, volume and inflections of voice, expressions, their smile, their reserve or extraversion.....it's not that hard to understand if you want to possess these skills. If you want to hire someone, it helps to use words that are valuable to them. If you don't want to hire someone, it helps to identify that and cut the meeting short.

I also have the ability to understand our agents with higher intelligence, and because of that, I'm more understanding of them. I like that I can say things like, "That's just Mary being a high **D.** *" It's a great tool for managing relationships better. You feel like you know people. It's almost like you have the upper hand.*

Leigh Giannotti
Merritt Island, FL

Johnny

The value of this information isn't just recognized by women. This letter is from a gentleman that immediately saw a difference in his relationship with his wife when he applied the information he learned at one of my seminars.

My wife and I love each other very much, but like any other couple, we have our moments of discontent. It was difficult for us to relate to one another at times. We thought it was just the way things were supposed to be. When I first took Angel's course, I said to myself many times, "That's my wife," and "There she is again." I have to tell you, it was an "aha" moment for me. My wife acted and reacted to my actions a certain way, and now I understood why. We're two different people. More importantly, I understand that I am responsible for my actions.

When money was tight, to me it wasn't a big deal, we would "get through it." But for her, it was terrible. Until Angel's seminar, I thought my wife was a worry wart. But now, I understand that part of her personality needs security, so I need to be sensitive and sympathetic to that.

Also, doing things at the last minute or springing things I planned without her was a large source of discontent. She is organized and likes to plan. I just like to go. We now have an online family calendar where we enter all of our events so that we are on the same page.

My wife also understands more about me and why I do what I do. When I would be excited about things, she would logic me to death and bring me down. She now shares my excitement at the beginning, and brings in logic slowly. I like that.

Now, don't get me wrong, we still have our moments of discontent, but man, they are much fewer!

Johnny Morrow
San Antonio, TX

Stephanie

This information is so valuable to businesses. Here's what one business owner, Stephanie, had to say:

I just wanted to send you a note to let you know that my agents and I really enjoyed your training. Everyone had a great time and, more importantly, everyone left with a better understanding on how to apply personality profiles to their businesses and everyday lives. Your training was the buzz in the office when we returned.

I have taken your training a couple of times and every time I learn something new. Thank you so much for your incredible program. We look forward to having you back in New Jersey again.

Stephanie Verderose

Vineland, NJ

Chuck

Evidently, the state of New Jersey recognizes the power of reading people. Here's another one.

Personality Profiles was a captivating event and I want to thank you for an exceptional and professional seminar. You are a true leader and clearly proficient in your field. Your elite presentation skills and knowledge of how to capture all personalities of the audience were remarkable.

Not only has your seminar made me a more efficient leader in my industry, it has made me a better communicator at home as well.

Understanding different personalities is crucial for sustaining and building healthy relationships with one's spouse, children, co-workers, and clients.

I am thankful for the opportunity to attend this life changing event for the second time. It's not typical that someone can capture and retain my attention for hours, and yet your class does just that. I look forward to having you back in New Jersey soon.

Chuck Hendershot
Bernardsville, NJ

Katrina

Katrina wrote to me after taking my seminar. Not only does this information change the lives of adults, but it can change the lives of children as well. This letter demonstrates the value of understanding our differences:

*My husband and I met you in Toronto. Your training definitely helped our relationship. I now understand why he does what he does, and he understands me. Plus, we now both understand how to communicate with our 4-year-old daughter. My husband is a **C/D** and I am a **D/I**. This training answered a lot of questions about our relationship and saved us numerous arguments that were simply misunderstandings. I think ALL couples should have this kind of training.*

Katrina Heldreth
Fredericksburg, VA

George

I especially love when men send me testimonials about how this has improved their lives. Here's a great one.

I want to thank you for the wonderful presentation of the DISC personality profiling system. It was both humorous and informative. Helping me to understand why I act the way I do was huge, and then getting me to laugh about myself was priceless!

When I got home from the seminar, my wife read my profile, and proclaimed, "This explains a lot!" Knowing why I act the way I do, and knowing how to recognize that not everyone is like me, has helped me to be more mindful of how to act around other people. I even used the material to profile my children.

I can't say that my family is operating under perfect peace and harmony, but at least now I understand why. I have also taken your "couples communication" course. Again, I can't say enough. My wife and I have been married for 16 years, and it was good to find out that we were not the only ones with communication issues.

I would recommend your classes to anyone!

George Guyott
Grand Rapids, MI

Laura

It just thrills me to know that people are using this information in their relationships. Here is a letter from Laura, who lives in Georgia.

After she took the seminar, she came back with her husband. What a difference it made.

I've taken Angel's seminar twice. The first time I attended, I found out why my husband gets so annoyed when I want details. What, when, where, how, who, why? He doesn't want to know details; they don't really matter to him. The bottom line is all he needs to hear.

The second time, I took my husband with me. It was an eye-opening experience. My husband said it was like a light bulb going off. Now we both understand that we are different personality types, and that has made a huge difference in our communication skills. I didn't think that was possible after 32 years of marriage. And if you want to mark jobs off the "honey do" list, well, it's all in how you ask.

The seminars were both great fun. It's a real laugh and learn experience.

Laura Parris
Locust Grove, GA

Scott and Laura

Here's a couple that understands the value of personality profiling. They only had one regret. Read on to discover what it was.

Personality profiles with Angel Tucker has helped us tremendously in our business by teaching us how to recognize a person's personality type so that we know the best way to present our business to them and how much information to give them. In sales, they teach you to sell to a person the way they want to be sold. But in order to do that effectively, it's imperative that you know that person's personality type.

Even more important, this training helps you in your own relationships. We are two very different personalities and, knowing what our differences are and why we respond or act a certain way, has gone a long way in strengthening and improving our marriage. We just wished we had this training when our kids were younger. It would have made our role as parents easier and I think we would have done a much better job raising them.

Angel's passion for what she does is evident in every course she teaches. She has a unique way of combining humor with education to make learning fun.

Scott and Laura Roussel

Searcy, AR

Loretta

Loretta really recognizes the value of using personality profiling in business. Here's what she had to say about the many times this information has benefited her company.

How can understanding personality profiles help your business? How can it not? Here's an example. I'm a real estate franchise owner, and one day I received an e-mail from a "for sale by owner" prospect. He had sent it out to the whole real estate community inviting them to his open house. I knew that most agents would be ticked off by this e-mail. I called one of my agents and told her to go to the open house *and just be herself. Afterward, she sent a handwritten note thanking him. As predicted, he was ready to list and called her for an interview. He informed her that he would also be interviewing other agents. She asked me how she could get an "edge. " We chatted about his house and she told me his closet was organized in shades of colors and very neat. We plugged his name into Facebook and saw his profession was "software engineer." He was a **C** without question. His wife was wearing a vibrant red shirt, smiling, had a lot of friends, and was involved in fundraising for the arts—a definite **I**. With the knowledge I gained from Angel's program, we developed a marketing plan that suited both of them. They were ecstatic. Unfortunately, they received an offer before the listing could occur, but when there was trouble with the offer and it looked like they would have to list, they called her right away. Preparing properly for a listing presentation and being able to give proper guidance to my agents are my biggest advantage.*

*Not only can understanding personality types improve your business, but they also enhance your personal relationships. Personally, I had two agents come to me on separate occasions complaining about not understanding their children. One agent is a high **D**. Her son was suffering from stress at school, headaches, and so on. I grabbed the phone and called Angel. She asked her some pointed questions, discovering that the child was an **S** and was constantly trying to please. She also sent a personality test for the child to complete and the whole family learned more about each other. Another example is a high **C** single parent I know. I got Angel on the phone and all I heard him say was, "You are describing my daughter to a tee." She is a **D** child* *and needed more challenges and options as she was feeling frustrated and bored.*

Isn't it amazing that this knowledge can change lives so much? Of all the training I have taken in my 19 years of real estate, this has been the easiest and most beneficial to apply and has given me a good grasp on my business that I never had before. I have learned so much from Angel's training.

Loretta Hughes

Regina, Saskatchewan, Canada

Bill

It's so heartwarming when I receive letters like this one.

*I'm a strong **D** type personality and was out of control. My wife, Karen, is a silent **S**. We had a good relationship and have always been very much in love. What we didn't know was how messed up our relationship was. Now, we are more in love than when we got married and are a shining example to all who know us.*

This training has also helped us with our nieces and nephew, our friends, and our co-workers. In business, this training paid for itself more times than we can count. We have gone through the training several times and look forward to attending every time we have the opportunity.

This is about relationships, and you can never know it all when it comes to them.

The books that Angel has written for children are such an important step in teaching children about the different types of personalities. This should be mandatory teaching in all schools from kindergarten all the way through high school.

Bill Farragher
Woodbridge, NJ

Michelle

Here's another business owner that sees the tremendous value of understanding about different personality types, and putting that to work in a company setting.

Angel's personality profile seminar was an amazing help in running a company on both the owner side, for interviewing people and seeing who would be a good fit in the office (or someone that would bring the rest down), as well as being able to better relate to clients' needs and understand why they were the way they were.

*I was also able to get my **D**-ness under control. People that wanted all the details drove me crazy, and I learned I needed to slow down and go at their speed. I had always realized that the purchase was not about me; however, by understanding the various types, I could quickly single out what personality they were and concentrate on what was important to them. Of course, Angel always makes training fun, exciting and non-stop laughs.*

Michelle Olson
Colorado Springs, CO

Scott

Scott truly understands the concept that personalities are simply different, and that each has something to contribute. Here's what he had to say.

Having learned the importance of, and differences in, our personalities from Angel Tucker, I have learned why we are how we are. No personality is wrong, just different. Different needs, different wants, different motivations.

By knowing the personalities of the people I direct and the clients I work with, I am able to provide a comfortable communication process that puts all parties in a comfort level with lower stress.

We have read the "Four Pals" books to each of three children, ages 8 to 14. After reading the stories, each kid can't wait to tell my wife and I which character they are, and especially which character their siblings are. The books make this understanding of personalities applicable to the young mind and begins the process of understanding that there are different personalities in everyone, and that's okay.

All of our agents are provided with a personality assessment upon joining our firm. This helps our management team, as well as the other staff, to understand our new addition. When we all know what motivates and drives us, we can communicate better, which adds to our positive and inviting office environment.

Scott Deaton

Little Rock, AR

Amie

Kudos to another person who sees the value of using this tool, not only in her business life but in her personal life as well. This is especially important when you're working with your spouse on a daily basis in the same business.

I was first introduced to personality profiles in 2004, when I attended Angel Tucker's course. The information I learned is priceless. Knowing my personality, and the personality of those that I come into contact with and have relationships with, has helped me both professionally and personally.

My husband and I are able to communicate with each other more effectively and understand the others' needs—especially since we are opposite personalities, which complement each other, but have caused us some serious problems, socially, since I am an **I** *and he is a* **C**.

In a professional setting, knowing and understanding how each personality type communicates, helps me to understand the needs of each of my clients and how I need to interact with them to get the best results out of our relationship. I have learned to interact with my children effectively as well. I have also been able to help my friends understand their children by sharing the information that I have learned. I am so thankful to understand the different personalities and how they affect our lives.

Amie Larsen
Salt Lake City, UT

Jean Marie

I love when parents apply this information to their relationships with their children. Here's what Jean Marie had to say that shows the value of making even small changes.

*Understanding personality types has changed the way I relate to my colleagues, friends, and family. Knowing my husband and daughter's personalities has made a huge difference in the way I parent. My daughter is a **D** and, at 10 years old, simply giving her a choice makes life so much easier. It is a choice I can live with and fills the need she has to be in control. That alone will change our lives forever!*

Jean Marie Grumbles
Franklin, TN

Steve

You can tell that Steve really "gets it" when it comes to personality profiling and it's benefits. Here's what he had to say in a recent e-mail to me.

Your class changed just about every aspect of our business. My wife and I work together and run an office. Prior to taking your class, we used to bump heads about anything and everything.

*The friction is gone now because we understand that we are two very different personality types (thank goodness). We now capitalize on our strengths and no longer have to deal with the weaknesses that caused the friction. A **D** and a **C** can really be complimentary.*

We also require every person in our office to complete a profile, which has allowed us to customize training and communications for each one. By knowing how to recognize personality types, we adjust presentations for clients and design marketing materials that attract the kinds of clients we love to work with.

Every business owner, employee, or manager can benefit from the skills you teach. We have taken the course twice and recommend it to every professional we know. This is a life skill, not just another class.

Steve Cramer

Denver, CO

Ish

I met Ish at a media event in New York City. Although he has never taken one of my seminars, he could tell just from a conversation how powerful profiling can be.

I had the good fortune of meeting Angel recently. She taught me more about my personality during the first fifteen minutes of meeting her than I had learned throughout years of my residency training. Angel profiled my personality with precision, poise, and good humor. As a psychiatrist, it's a rarity that I meet someone with not only keen insight but also practical application in the field of personalities. Thanks Angel!

Ish Major, M.D.

South Carolina

Mom and daughter

I can tell you story after story about people who have had life-changing experiences. Often, they come up to me in tears of thankfulness.

Recently, I was speaking at an engagement in Georgia. A young woman came up to me during the break and said, "I just want to thank you for saving the relationship between my mother and I." She explained that her mother is a **C** and she is an **I**, so all her life, her mother thought her daughter had something wrong with her. It was such a revelation to find out they were just different. The young woman shared with me how this new understanding changed her mother's opinion of her and, therefore, her acceptance. Furthermore, she said, she felt better equipped to be a mother when she has kids of her own. This is the type of story that keeps me on airplanes week after week.

Universal challenges

Can you see yourself in any of these stories? They are universal. They are the same challenges that each of us deal with every day— communication, misunderstandings, and confusion. The information in this book is the very same information that each of these people found to be life changing. I know you will as well.

CHAPTER 18

Putting It All Into Practice

Now that you have learned about the different personality types, this chapter will give you practical ways to apply what you've learned. It also contains some exercises that help you put personality profiling into practice. Additionally, you'll see some great examples of how the personality types respond differently to the same situation.

The most important thing to keep in mind when using the personality profiling tool is exactly that... it's a tool. If you do not use it, you will not reap the rewards. Just imagine driving a nail into a wall using your hand instead of hammer. It's going to be much more difficult—and painful—than it would be if you used the right tool. It's the same with profiling. You must use the tool to reap its benefits.

Pay attention

The biggest challenge with using the profiling tool is that it requires you to pay attention to others. The reality is, you usually pay attention only to you (as we all do). You must practice taking the focus off of yourself and putting it on to other people so you can become an effective profiler.

You made your bed (or not), now you can just lie in it

Did you notice at least one trait in each of the four personality types that sounded like you? That is the way that it should be. As I said, you contain all four personalities in you. Depending upon how much you have of that type determines how much you related to. You will have at least one "thing" that you do in each group.

As I mentioned, my husband is an **S/I** blend. Since he's in the Air Force, we move quite often. Because he is an **S/I**, it would be fine with him to live out of boxes until we move again—*as long as the bed is made.* A made up bed is his **C** thing.

I'm a high **D/I** blend, so I don't make the bed. To me, it's a waste of time. After all, I'm going to get right back in it again at the end of the day. Unless I have company coming over and they are going to see my bedroom, what is the point?

I can still remember when we first got married. I would be sleeping when my husband left for work, and he would try to make the bed around me—while I was still in it. As I felt the sheets being tucked underneath me, I'm thinking, "What? Does he think I am going to stay like this the rest of the day?" Luckily, I persuaded him to stop doing this pretty quickly.

For the record bed makers, research shows that you have much less of those nice little mites that eat your dead skin at night if you don't make the bed. When you make the bed, it keeps them nice and cozy—and breeding. When you don't make the bed, they get cold and die. Just another good reason *not* to make the bed.

Campout

Since I mentioned the military, now would be a great time to tell you a little story. This story shows how a **C** and a **D** respond differently in the same situation. Two military guys were out in the woods on a special assignment. They were sharing a tent as they slept. When they awoke the next morning, the **D** asked the **C**, "What do you see?"

The **C** replied, "I see a beautiful blue sky. I see a cardinal feeding her babies in the tree about 50 yards to our left. I also see a stream in the distance." He went on and on in detail about what he observed. When he was done, he turned to the **D** and asked, "What do you see?"

The **D** replied, "I see someone stole our tent."

Recognizing traits

By recognizing one trait about a person, you can begin to know how to communicate with them so you can create win-win situations.

Let's say that you notice that a person is finding it hard to relax, or maybe that they are talking with their hands often. That person is one of two personality types: a **D** or an **I**. Here's how this information helps you. You now know that they are going to be bottom line, move fast, and make quick decisions. Even if you don't know which one of the two types they are, you still know how to begin helping them. How cool is that?

The hands say it all

Speaking of hands, if you get really good at observing people, you can determine what personality type they are by the way they move their hands. **D**'s make very short, blunt, authoritative movements. The hand movements of an **I** are much more animated, expressive, big, and flowing.

Same story, different reactions

I'm going to tell you a story. Afterwards, I'm going to explain how each of the four personality types would react to it.

One day, an 8-year-old boy was in the local grocery store with his mother. When they got to the check-out counter, the boy spots a very large jar of M&Ms on the counter. The cashier notices the little boy eyeing the candy. Here's how the conversation went:

Cashier: Would you like some M&Ms?

Boy: (excitedly) Yes!

Cashier: Go ahead and grab a handful.

Boy: Nope.

Cashier: (confused) I thought you said you wanted some.

Boy: I do.

Cashier: Then take a handful. Go ahead.

Boy: No, thanks.

Cashier   (puzzled) Well, do you want me to get them for you?

Boy: Yes!

Once mother and son left the store, the mother asked, "Why didn't you want to get the candy yourself? The boy replied. "His hand is a lot bigger than mine."

Here are the different reactions:

- The **D** thinks, "That's pretty smart. That's exactly what I would've done. The kid must be a **D**."
- The **I** didn't bother reading the whole story. He or she stopped to dream about M&Ms, thinking, "I love M&Ms, especially blue ones. I wonder if they were plain or peanut."
- The **S** thinks, "That is so sweet for that man to have candy available for the kids. He probably paid for it himself. What a nice guy."
- The **C** thinks, "I hope that mom is not going to let her son eat those M&Ms after that man had his nasty, germy hand all over that candy."

Isn't it interesting how all of the personalities approach the same situation in very different ways?

What type of driver are you?

You can also tell someone's personality by the way they drive their car.

- **D**'s are tailgaters. And they weave in and out of traffic. They may not know that their car comes with an optional feature called a blinker.
- **I**'s like to look at their passenger while driving. They run red lights, go through stop signs, and pass their exits on the interstate. They also slow down and speed up for no apparent reason to anyone else around them.
- **S**-types have never been in a wreck—but they have been the cause of many. It takes them about 20 minutes to merge onto a busy highway (okay, not really 20, but it seems like it to everyone around them).

- C's are the best drivers. They obey every rule of the road and use their blinker at precisely the right time, according to the instructions in driver's manual.

Pilots and personalities

Do you ever fly on a plane? This is a great exercise. Try to determine the personality of the pilot. Captains **D**, **I**, **S**, and **C** are all very different.

Captain D

A **D** pilot often makes announcements right after you take off and right before you land. He may sound a little bit rude, as if you are an intrusion on him. He's probably thinking something like, "I am the most important person on this plane. I'm kind of busy, but they tell me you need to know all this stuff, so here you go."

The first time I flew after September 11th, I had a **D** pilot. How did I know? He took the microphone away from the flight attendant and said, "I used to let the flight attendants make the announcements, but now I do it. The cushion you're on is a flotation device, but it will also protect you against a two-inch knife. If you see anyone dressed like me coming towards this cabin, attack them, because I *will* land this plane on the ground." I later learned his nickname was Mad Dog.

Captain I

I pilots are often out front welcoming the passengers. They are the ones who show kids the cockpit and give them little airplane wings or cards with pictures of the plane. Years ago, they would come out of the cockpit on long flights and talk with the passengers about sports, or whatever else interested them. (This really freaks **S** passengers, out by the way.)

Captain S

An **S** pilot is the most soothing. He may say something like, "Sit back and relax. We're here to serve you. It's a beautiful day and it's going to be a smooth ride. Your comfort and safety are very important to us. Please let us know if there is anything we can do to make you feel more comfortable."

Captain C

The **C** pilots tend to be the most annoying to me. Every fifteen minutes or so they tell you how high you are flying, what state you are flying over, what the temperature is outside, and any historical information that they find fascinating.

If you are a **C** passenger on that plane, you are in heaven. You think, "What excellent information!"

As a **D**, I think, "I have no intention of going outside this plane right now, so I really don't care what the temperature is. That's useless information. Please quit interrupting and let me finish watching the movie. Don't disturb me unless the plane's wing is on fire."

Who's the co-pilot?

Recently, I was on a plane with a high **I** pilot. He was out front welcoming all the passengers and making jokes with each one as they came in. Normally, this isn't a concern for me, but we were already late taking off. I wondered if he would forget where the controls were in the cockpit.

I asked the flight attendant if I could meet the co-pilot. She said, "Sure, but just to let you know, he's a very quiet guy." I replied, "That's all I need to know." That means he was either an **S** or **C**—either one worked for me. I instantly felt much safer.

Lather, rinse, repeat

That is what most bottles of shampoo have as their directions. Here is how the four personality types respond:

- **D**'s say, "Don't tell me what to do! I'll lather just once, thank you."
- **I**'s say "Lather, rinse, repeat. Got it. Oops, did I already repeat? I can't remember."
- **S**-types and **C**'s say, "Okay, if those are the rules then that's what I'll do."

Our personalities dictate the way we wash our hair, deal a deck of cards, wash clothes—everything.

Planning time together

As I mentioned, my husband is an **I/S** blend. In my experience, it's very difficult to plan a vacation with this personality blend. First, he has no concept of time and wants to do everything spontaneously (**I**), and second, he doesn't really care if things go as planned (**S**). As a **D**, I want complete control (surprise, surprise).

Several years ago, we went to Seattle on vacation and to attend a wedding. We were going to have only a few days of fun time and there is so much to do there. When we talked about this, my husband said, "Let's just put five things on the list for each day. If we don't get to everything on the list, that's okay." Well as a **D**, if a list exists, I'm going to check off everything on it *and* slip in a bonus task. If an item says, "Go to the zoo," I would go to the entrance of the zoo and mark it off the list. After all, the list didn't say go *in* the zoo, it said *to* the zoo.

As a compromise, we put three things on the list for each day. We knew we could easily do three, and anything beyond that would be a bonus. See? Opposites really can live happily together, as long as you work with each other's comfort levels.

Easily influenced

There are two personality types that you can talk into just about anything—if you have their attention long enough. They are the **I**'s and the **S**-types. These two types both make decisions based on emotion, so if you get the emotion right, they will buy into whatever it is you're trying to sell them.

My husband makes me laugh because his **S** side keeps him from wanting to spend money or make changes, but once he's in the store, his **I** side wants to buy everything in sight. He gets excited over gadgets and freebies.

Just recently, a company was selling car wax in the store parking lot of the military base where he's stationed. They were set up there for quite a while. Every time I went to the store, I purposely parked in a location to avoid the car wax salespeople.

A few weeks later, I was looking for something in the garage and found— you guessed it—car wax. Not just one can, but six cans. As a **D**, I'm logical and realistic, and I know he's never going to have time to use it on the cars. I asked my husband why he bought them. He said, "It was a good deal."

Office space

Even at work, personalities operate differently. You can often figure out a personality type by their offices.

- **D**'s and **I**'s have what I call "I love *me*" walls hung with plaques and certificates that show their accomplishments.

- **S**-types have pictures of their family, homemade cards, and drawings from their kids pinned on every surface of their cubicles.

- **C**'s have an office that is structured. Everything has a specific place and everything is orderly and efficient.

What say you?

Now let's have some fun. Below are 15 sayings. Your job is to see if you can figure out which personality would say them. The answers will follow.

1. Measure twice, cut once.
2. Hill? What hill? I don't remember any hill?
3. Sit back, relax.
4. Cleanliness is next to Godliness.
5. Working together, we can do it.
6. I like long walks, especially when they're taken by people who annoy me.
7. The party doesn't start till I get there!
8. Lack of planning on your part does not constitute an emergency on my part.

9. If you can't be with the one you love, just love the one you're with.

10. We were all put on this earth to goof off, and don't let anyone tell you any different.

11. If I want your opinion, I'll ask for it.

12. It's my way or the highway.

13. If it's worth doing, it's worth doing right.

14. If I agreed with you, then we'd both be wrong.

15. Mrs. Clean lives here.

Do you think you got them all right? Let's find out. Here are the answers:

1. C	6. D	11. D
2. I	7. I	12. D
3. S	8. C*	13. C
4. C	9. I	14. D
5. S	10. I	15. C

*C's are the only ones that would use the word "constitute."

So how'd you do? If you didn't get them all, you may want to review this book again.

List makers

Remember how I said that **D**'s and **I**'s are bottom line and **S**-types and **C**'s are A to Z? This shows up in the way they make lists. For example, when I make a list to remind me of what I need to do, as a **D**, I write one word. It looks something like:

- Drawer
- Garage
- Closet

When my **S** husband makes a list to remind him of the same tasks, it looks something like:

- Clean out top drawer in bathroom so wallet and keys will fit in
- Re-arrange boxes in garage so they fit on shelves
- Organize closet in master bedroom

Pretty amazing, don't you think?

Move on

Sometimes people think, "I don't think I can work with a particular personality." My answer is, then don't. Refer them to someone who can. You're probably going to lose them any way. It's better to collect a referral fee on a business deal than to lose the customer altogether. A percentage of something is better than 100 percent of nothing.

Before you do this, however, decide whether you truly *can't* work with this person or is it more that you don't *want* to work with him or her. These are two very different things.

Some advice: Life is going to put people in our paths that we prefer not to work with. If we constantly choose not to work with them, are we really growing as a person? Are we sharpening our profiling skills? Probably not. Don't focus on the action, focus on the result.

A final thought

I want to leave you with this thought. Every personality type has something to offer. Everyone is capable of accomplishing great things in this world.

I love the story about a little boy who was in the park. He saw a man holding a handful of balloons that were for sale. As the little boy watched, the man accidentally let go of a red balloon. The boy walked up to the man.

Boy: Sir, if you let go of a black balloon will it go just as high as the red one?"

Man: Yes.

Boy: Sir, if you let go of a white balloon, will it go as high as the red one and the black one?"

Man: (annoyed) Of course.

Boy: Sir, if you let go of the yellow balloon, will it go as high as the others?"

Man: (frustrated) It doesn't matter what color the balloon is on the outside, it's the stuff on the inside that makes it rise!"

How true that is with us as well. It doesn't matter your color, your personality, your social status, your whatever. It's what's on the inside of you that makes a difference.

I encourage *you* to make a difference. Don't know where to start? How about starting by sharing this book with someone you know. Give them the power of understanding others. Maybe even buy them their own copy. In fact, give a copy to friends, family, co-workers, and anyone else you have a relationship with. This information can be life changing for all who embrace it.

What better gift could you give someone than that?

Recommended Reading

Not only do we have differences between personalities, but there are differences between genders as well. Men and women process information and handle situations differently. This book is not meant to address these differences, so I highly recommend reading the book, *Men are from Mars and Women are from Venus*, by Dr. John Gray. It's a huge eye-opener. I have not found another book that clearly explains the gender differences like this one. Check it out. It could improve your relationships with the opposite gender greatly.

If you are a parent, I highly recommend getting a copy of *Personality Insights For Moms*. (I mentioned this book in Chapter 16 as well.) This award-winning book was written by a good friend of mine named Susan Crook. It's an awesome read and will help any parent. If you don't have kids, you probably know someone that does, so consider giving this as a gift for Mother's Day, to a new mommy as a baby shower gift, or for any other occasion.

As I've mentioned, there are a number of great resources available on my Web site. Go to **www.personalityprofiles.org** and click on "Order Materials" to see all of the books, CDs, and other products. You will automatically receive a ten percent discount at checkout for ordering from my Web site.

Finally, help me to help others. World Vision is an international organization that helps underprivileged children all over the world. I personally support this organization, and would love if you did, too. In fact, there are some free goodies just for helping. Go to my Web site, **www.personalityprofiles.org**, and click on "World Vision" to get more information or to adopt a child.

I so enjoy receiving notes and letters in the mail from my adopted child. It's like a little gift every time they arrive. I urge you to give yourself a gift like this, too. For the price of a few large pizzas every month, you can change the life of a child. How easy is that?

There is also a place on my site to make a donation so that needy children around the world can receive my children's books for free. Won't you consider making a donation? One hundred percent of the proceeds go to buying books for needy children to give them the gift of understanding each other's different personalities. Just look for the "Donate Books" button on my Web site.

About the Author

Angel Tucker is a certified human behavior consultant who has been teaching personality profiles for over 20 years. She is also the creator and award-winning author of the *Four Pals* children's book series. Additionally, she has been featured in magazines and articles as an Expert Profiler, and has been on numerous radio talk shows.

If you are interested in having Angel speak at an engagement, please go to **www.personalityprofiles.org** and complete the "Contact Us" page. Your inquiry will be responded to promptly.

CPSIA information can be obtained at www.ICGtesting.com
Printed in the USA
BVOW05s1647081014

369942BV00001B/4/P